THE
TOP 100
QUICK & EASY
SAUCES

THE
TOP 100
QUICK & EASY
SAUCES

MOUTHWATERING CLASSIC AND CONTEMPORARY RECIPES

Anne Sheasby

DUNCAN BAIRD PUBLISHERS

LONDON

The Top 100 Quick & Easy Sauces
Anne Sheasby

Distributed in the USA and Canada by
Sterling Publishing Co., Inc.
387 Park Avenue South
New York, NY 10016-8810

This edition first published in the UK and USA in 2010 by
Duncan Baird Publishers Ltd
Sixth Floor, Castle House
75–76 Wells Street
London W1T 3QH

Copyright © Duncan Baird Publishers 2005, 2010
Text copyright © Anne Sheasby 2005, 2010
Photography copyright © Duncan Baird Publishers 2005,
2010

The right of Anne Sheasby to be identified as the Author of
this text has been asserted in accordance with the Copyright,
Designs and Patents Act of 1988.

Managing Editor: Grace Cheetham
Editor: Alison Bolus
Managing Designer: Manisha Patel
Designer: Luana Gobbo
Commissioned photography: William Lingwood, Simon Smith
and Toby Scott
Food Stylist: Lucy McKelvie
Prop Stylist: Helen Trent

Library of Congress Cataloging-in-Publication Data

Sheasby, Anne.
  The top 100 quick & easy sauces : mouthwatering classic
and contemporary recipes / Anne Sheasby.
    p. cm.
  Includes index.
  ISBN 978-1-84483-906-3
  1. Sauces. I. Title. II. Title: Top one hundred quick and
easy sauces.
  TX819.S54 2010
  641.8'14--dc22
                        2009042884

ISBN: 978-1-84483-906-3

10 9 8 7 6 5 4 3 2 1

Typeset in News Gothic
Color reproduction by Colourscan
Printed in Malaysia for Imago

For information about custom editions, special sales,
premium and corporate purchases, please contact
Sterling Special Sales Department at 800-805-5489 or
specialsales@sterlingpub.com.

Publisher's Note
While every care has been taken in compiling the recipes for
this book, Duncan Baird Publishers, or any other persons
who have been involved in working on this publication,
cannot accept responsibility for any errors or omissions,
inadvertent or not, that may be found in the recipes or text,
nor for any problems that may arise as a result of preparing
one of these recipes. If you are pregnant or breastfeeding or
have any special dietary requirements or medical conditions,
it is advisable to consult a medical professional before
following any of the recipes contained in this book.

Notes on the Recipes
Unless otherwise stated:
Use extra-large eggs, and medium fruit and vegetables
Use fresh ingredients, including herbs
1 tsp. = 5ml 1 tbsp. = 15ml 1 cup = 240ml
• Some of the recipes in this book contain raw or lightly
cooked eggs—these recipes are not recommended for babies
and young children, pregnant women, the elderly, and those
convalescing.

CONTENTS

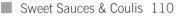

SAUCE BASICS

A good sauce can provide the finishing touch to many dishes, complementing and enhancing the flavor of the most simple food without being overpowering. A grilled steak, chicken portion, or fish steak can be transformed into something really special with the addition of a good sauce. Sauces not only add flavor and color to dishes, they also add texture and moisture, and there is a whole variety to suit all tastes and palates—savory and sweet, rich and light, hot and cold.

TYPES OF SAUCES

There are several types of sauce, including roux-based, brown, or emulsified sauces, vegetable-based sauces, and purees, gravies, and flavored butters, as well as salsas, relishes, salad dressings and vinaigrettes, and savory and sweet dips, plus sweet sauces, fruit purees, and coulis.

ROUX-BASED SAUCES

A roux is a blend of equal quantities of melted butter and all-purpose flour that are cooked together before liquid, such as milk or stock, is gradually stirred or whisked into it over gentle heat to make a béchamel sauce. Once the sauce has come to a boil and thickened, it is left to simmer gently 2 to 3 minutes to cook out the taste of the flour.

With a classic White or Béchamel Sauce, the roux is cooked but not colored, whereas for brown sauces, such as Espagnole (Brown) Sauce, the roux is cooked until it becomes brown.

EMULSIFIED SAUCES

Emulsified sauces are based on one of two emulsions—a butter emulsion, such as Hollandaise Sauce or Beurre Blanc; or a cold emulsion of oil and egg yolks, such as Mayonnaise. With a butter emulsion, the initial cooking liquid used for the sauce is reduced during cooking to give a more intense flavor to the sauce, which is then enriched and thickened with butter or eggs.

FRUIT PUREES AND COULIS

These are simple to make and create a delicious fruit sauce to accompany desserts, such as fresh fruit, ice cream, or meringues, as well as adding a lovely visual finishing touch. Fruit coulis are made by first pureeing raw or lightly cooked fruit. The puree is then sieved, sweetened, and sometimes flavored with liqueur, to give a delicious and colorful pouring sauce.

Fruits such as raspberries, strawberries, mixed berries, mangoes, peaches, and apricots are ideal for making fruit coulis. Some fruit- or vegetable-based sauces can also be thickened by blending the ingredients together using a stick blender, or a small blender or food processor.

THICKENING SAUCES

Sauces can be thickened in various ways at different stages of a recipe. Sometimes a sauce is thickened at the beginning of a recipe with a roux, or toward the end of a recipe using egg yolks, butter, or cream. Another thickener that is added toward the end of the preparation time is beurre manié—equal quantities of softened butter and all-purpose flour kneaded together to make a smooth paste, which is then whisked into the hot sauce or liquid until it thickens.

Sauces can also be thickened using cornstarch, arrowroot, or potato flour blended with a little cold milk or water, then added to the sauce and heated, while stirring, until the sauce comes to a boil and thickens. Serve sauces thickened with arrowroot or potato flour as soon as they have thickened—if they are allowed to simmer for more than 1 minute or so, they can become thin again. Sauces thickened with cornstarch need to be simmered 2 to 3 minutes.

REDUCING SAUCES

An alternative method of thickening sauces is to boil the mixture rapidly until it reduces in volume. Do not season the sauce until it is reduced, as reducing intensifies the flavors. Once the sauce has reduced, skim off any froth from the surface using a slotted or metal spoon. Do not attempt to reduce a sauce containing eggs or yogurt by this method as it is likely to curdle. Quick cream sauces can usually be reduced in this way, but those using crème fraîche might curdle.

Chapter 1

BASIC & CLASSIC SAUCES

Basic sauces are an important element of everyday cooking. This chapter brings together a wide selection of good, basic sauces, such as Basic White Sauce, Rich Cheese Sauce, and Béarnaise Sauce, each of which can be served simply, perhaps with meat, fish, or vegetables. Other essential, sauces, such as Rich Tomato Sauce, which can be used as the basis for tempting recipes, such as meat or vegetable lasagnes, are also included.

Many of the classic sauces, such as Mayonnaise, Aïoli, and Herby Lemon Hollandaise, will be familiar to you, although perhaps you have not tried to make them before, while others, such as Velouté Sauce, Bordelaise Sauce, and Saffron Sauce, might be less familiar. Once you have mastered a few easy techniques, you can enjoy creating a whole range of classic sauces at home, and you will never want to go back to store-bought products again.

Herby Lemon Hollandaise (see page 27)

001 Basic White Sauce (Pouring Sauce)

PREPARATION TIME 5 minutes **COOKING TIME** 10 minutes **SERVES** 4

1 tbsp. butter

1 tbsp. all-purpose flour

1¼ cups milk

salt and freshly ground black pepper

1 Melt the butter in a small saucepan, stir in the flour, and cook, stirring, 1 minute. Remove the pan the pan from the heat and gradually stir or whisk in the milk.

2 Return the pan to the heat and bring slowly to a boil, stirring or whisking until the sauce is thick and smooth. Simmer slowly 2 to 3 minutes, stirring continuously. Season to taste with salt and pepper. Serve hot.

SERVING SUGGESTIONS Serve with hot slices of baked ham or broiled chicken breasts. Alternatively, serve with broiled fillets of flounder or sole, or with cooked fava or green beans.

002 Creamy White Wine Sauce

PREPARATION TIME 10 minutes   **COOKING TIME** 20 minutes   **SERVES** 4 to 6

¾ cup dry white wine
¾ cup heavy cream
5 tbsp. fish or vegetable stock (homemade
    or from a bouillon cube)

1 tbsp. chopped dill or chervil (optional)
1 tbsp. chopped parsley
salt and freshly ground black pepper

1 Pour the wine into a saucepan, bring to a boil, and boil rapidly until it reduces by half.
2 Stir in the cream and stock and bring back to a boil, then reduce the heat and simmer,
    uncovered, 10 to 15 minutes, or until the sauce is slightly thicker, stirring occasionally.
3 Remove the pan from the heat and stir in the dill, if using, and parsley. Season to taste with
    salt and pepper. Serve hot.

SERVING SUGGESTIONS Serve with broiled, baked, or pan-fried whole flounder or lemon sole or with
pan-fried perch fillets.

003 Rich Cheese Sauce

PREPARATION TIME 10 minutes   **COOKING TIME** 10 minutes   **SERVES** 4

1 tbsp. butter

1 tbsp. all-purpose flour

1¼ cups whole milk

¾ cup grated sharp cheddar cheese

2 tbsp. freshly grated Parmesan cheese

1 tsp. Dijon mustard

freshly grated nutmeg, to taste (optional)

salt and freshly ground black pepper

1 Melt the butter in a small saucepan, stir in the flour, and cook, stirring, 1 minute. Remove the pan from the heat and gradually stir or whisk in the milk.

2 Return the pan to the heat and bring slowly to a boil, stirring or whisking until the sauce is thick and smooth.

3 Stir in the cheeses and mustard and cook over low heat 5 minutes, or until the cheeses melt and the sauce is smooth and glossy, stirring continuously. Season to taste with salt and pepper, and a little nutmeg, if using. Serve hot.

SERVING SUGGESTIONS Serve with oven-baked ham, or with broiled cod or halibut. Alternatively, serve with cooked cauliflower or broccoli florets, or with hot gnocchi or macaroni.

VARIATIONS Use Swiss or Monterey Jack cheese in place of cheddar and Parmesan. Use prepared English mustard in place of Dijon mustard.

004 Béarnaise Sauce

PREPARATION TIME 10 minutes   COOKING TIME 15 minutes   SERVES 4 to 6

3 tbsp. tarragon or white-wine vinegar
½ tsp. black peppercorns
2 shallots, finely chopped
a few tarragon sprigs
1 bay leaf
2 egg yolks

1 stick butter, at room temperature, diced
1 to 2 tbsp. chopped mixed herbs, such as
    tarragon, parsley, and chervil
freshly squeezed lemon juice, to taste
    (optional)
salt and freshly ground black pepper

1 Put the vinegar in a small saucepan with the peppercorns, shallots, tarragon sprigs, bay leaf, and 1 tablespoon water. Bring to a boil, then lower the heat and simmer until the mixture reduces to about 1 tablespoon liquid. Remove the pan from the heat and set aside.

2 Put the egg yolks in a heatproof bowl with 1 tablespoon of the butter and a pinch of salt and beat together using a balloon whisk. Strain the reduced vinegar into the egg mixture and stir to mix.

3 Put the bowl over a pan of barely simmering water and whisk the egg mixture about 4 minutes, until it is pale and beginning to thicken.

4 Gradually whisk in the remaining butter, one piece at a time, until the mixture begins to thicken and emulsify. Make sure each piece of butter is incorporated into the sauce before adding the next piece.

5 Once all the butter has been added and the sauce is light and thick, remove the bowl from the heat and whisk 1 minute. Stir in the herbs and season with salt and pepper to taste. Add a small squeeze of lemon juice, if desired. Serve immediately.

SERVING SUGGESTIONS Serve with broiled cod or salmon steaks. Alternatively, serve with broiled or pan-fried beef steaks, or with steamed asparagus, green beans, or baby zucchini.

005 Velouté Sauce

PREPARATION TIME 5 minutes   **COOKING TIME** 10 minutes   **SERVES** 4 to 6

4 tsp. butter
3 tbsp. all-purpose flour
1¼ cups chicken, fish, vegetable,
    or meat stock (homemade
    or from a bouillon cube)

2 tbsp. heavy cream
½ tsp. freshly squeezed lemon juice
salt and freshly ground black pepper

1 Melt the butter in a small saucepan, stir in the flour, and cook, stirring, about 2 minutes,
   or until light golden in color. Remove the pan from the heat and gradually stir or whisk
   in the stock.
2 Return the pan to the heat and bring slowly to a boil, stirring or whisking until the sauce
   is thick and smooth. Simmer 2 to 3 minutes, stirring continuously.
3 Stir in the cream, then stir in the lemon juice. Season to taste with salt and pepper. Serve hot.

SERVING SUGGESTIONS Serve with broiled or roasted chicken breasts, or cod or flounder fillets.
Alternatively, serve with broiled pork chops.

006 Rich Tomato Sauce

PREPARATION TIME 5 minutes   COOKING TIME 45 minutes   SERVES 4 to 6

3 tbsp. butter
1 red onion, finely chopped
2 garlic cloves, crushed
2 cans (15-oz.) crushed tomatoes
⅔ cup red wine

2 tbsp. tomato paste
½ tsp. sugar
1 bouquet garni
salt and freshly ground black pepper

1 Melt the butter in a saucepan, add the onion and garlic, and fry slowly 10 minutes, or until soft, stirring occasionally.
2 Add the tomatoes, wine, tomato paste, sugar, and bouquet garni and mix well. Bring to a boil, then lower the heat and simmer, uncovered, about 30 minutes, until the sauce is thick and pulpy, stirring occasionally.
3 Discard the bouquet garni and season to taste with salt and pepper. Serve hot.

SERVING SUGGESTIONS Serve with hot pasta, such as tagliatelle or fusilli, or use as the basis for a vegetable or meat lasagne. Alternatively, serve with meatballs or cooked vegetables.

007 Barbecue Sauce

PREPARATION TIME 10 minutes   **COOKING TIME** 20 minutes   **SERVES** 4 to 6

2 tbsp. butter

1 red onion, finely chopped

1 can (15-oz.) crushed tomatoes

4 tbsp. light beer

1 tbsp. red-wine vinegar

1 tbsp. Worcestershire sauce

1 tbsp. tomato paste

1 tbsp. light soft brown sugar

2 tsp. Dijon mustard

salt and freshly ground black pepper

1 Melt the butter in a saucepan, add the onion and fry gently 5 minutes, or until soft.

2 Add the tomatoes, beer, vinegar, Worcestershire sauce, tomato paste, sugar, and mustard and stir to mix well.

3 Bring slowly to a boil, stirring, then lower the heat and simmer, uncovered, 10 to 15 minutes, until the sauce is slightly thicker, stirring occasionally. Season to taste with salt and pepper. Serve hot.

SERVING SUGGESTIONS Serve with barbecued vegetable, chicken kabobs, or chicken drumsticks.

008 Soubise (Onion) Sauce

PREPARATION TIME 10 minutes   COOKING TIME 20 minutes   SERVES 4

3 tbsp. butter
1 large onion, finely chopped
2 tbsp. all-purpose flour

1¼ cups milk
salt and freshly ground black pepper

1 Melt half of the butter in a saucepan, add the onion and fry 10 to 15 minutes, or until soft.
Remove the pan from the heat and set aside.

2 Melt the remaining butter in a separate saucepan, stir in the flour and cook 1 minute, stirring.
Remove the pan from the heat and gradually stir or whisk in the milk.

3 Return the pan to the heat and bring slowly to a boil, stirring or whisking until the sauce
is thick and smooth. Leave to simmer 2 to 3 minutes, stirring continuously.

4 Stir in the fried onion and reheat slowly until hot, stirring continuously. Season to taste with salt
and pepper. Serve hot.

SERVING SUGGESTIONS Serve with baked ham or roast chicken, or with broiled haddock or monkfish.
VARIATION Use 1 large red onion in place of the yellow onion.
COOK'S TIP Leave the root end intact when slicing or chopping an onion. This prevents the release of the
strong juices and fumes that cause eyes to water.

009 Creamy Mushroom Sauce

PREPARATION TIME 10 minutes   **COOKING TIME** 15 minutes   **SERVES** 4 to 6

⅔ cup vegetable stock (homemade or from a bouillon cube)
1¼ cups heavy cream
3 tbsp. butter
2½ cups sliced cremini mushrooms
1½ cups sliced button mushrooms
1 to 2 tbsp. chopped mixed herbs, such as parsley, chives, and marjoram or oregano
salt and freshly ground black pepper

1 Pour the stock and cream into a saucepan. Bring slowly to a boil, then lower the heat and simmer until the sauce is thick enough to coat the back of a wooden spoon, stirring frequently.

2 Meanwhile, melt the butter in a skillet, add all the mushrooms, and fry 5 minutes, or until soft. Increase the heat slightly and cook, stirring frequently, until all the liquid evaporates.

3 Add the mushrooms and herbs to the cream sauce and reheat slowly until hot, stirring continuously. Season to taste with salt and pepper. Serve hot.

SERVING SUGGESTIONS Serve with broiled chicken breasts or pan-fried steaks. Alternatively, serve with baked cod or haddock fillets, or broiled tuna steaks.
VARIATIONS Use crème fraîche or sour cream in place of heavy cream. Use mixed wild mushrooms in place of the cremini mushrooms.

010 Bordelaise Sauce

PREPARATION TIME 10 minutes   **COOKING TIME** 1 hour 15 minutes   **SERVES** 4 to 6

2 tbsp. butter
1 slice Canadian bacon, finely chopped
2 shallots, finely chopped
1 carrot, finely chopped
⅔ cup finely chopped mushrooms
3 tbsp. all-purpose flour

1¼ cups beef stock (homemade or from
   a bouillon cube)
1¼ cups red wine
1 bouquet garni
salt and freshly ground black pepper

1 Melt the butter in a saucepan. Add the bacon and cook 2 minutes, stirring. Add the shallots, carrot, and mushrooms and fry gently 8 minutes, or until soft and light brown.
2 Stir in the flour and cook, stirring, until the flour is light brown. Remove the pan from the heat and gradually stir or whisk in the stock and wine. Return the pan to the heat and bring slowly to a boiland cook until the mixture thickens, stirring continously. Add the bouquet garni and salt and pepper to taste. Cover and simmer 1 hour, stirring occasionally.
3 Remove the pan from the heat and let cool slightly, then strain the sauce through a sieve. Discard the contents of the sieve. Return the strained sauce to the rinsed-out pan and reheat slowly before serving. Adjust the seasoning to taste. Serve hot.

SERVING SUGGESTIONS Serve with pan-fried filet mignons or other steaks, or with roast lamb or pheasant.
VARIATION Use smoked bacon in place of unsmoked bacon.

011 Parsley Sauce

PREPARATION TIME 5 minutes   COOKING TIME 10 minutes   SERVES 4

1 tbsp. butter
1 tbsp. all-purpose flour
1¼ cups milk

2 to 3 tbsp. chopped parsley
salt and freshly ground black pepper

1 Melt the butter in a small saucepan, stir in the flour, and cook, stirring, 1 minute. Remove the pan from the heat and gradually stir or whisk in the milk.

2 Return the pan to the heat and bring slowly to a boil, stirring or whisking until the sauce is thick and smooth. Simmer 2 to 3 minutes, stirring continuously.

3 Stir in the parsley and season to taste with salt and pepper. Serve hot.

SERVING SUGGESTIONS Serve with broiled cod, or haddock fillets. Alternatively, serve with baked glazed ham, or with cooked fava beans, baby corn cobs, or spinach.
VARIATIONS Use ⅔ cup vegetable stock or heavy cream in place of ⅔ cup of the milk. Use 1 to 2 tablespoons chopped mixed herbs in place of parsley.
COOK'S TIP For a thicker Parsley Sauce, simply follow the recipe above but increase the quantities of butter to 2 tablespoons and flour to 1½ tablespoons.

012 Saffron Sauce

PREPARATION TIME 20 minutes, plus soaking   **COOKING TIME** 20 minutes   **SERVES** 4

½ tsp. saffron strands

3 tbsp. chilled butter, diced

2 shallots, finely chopped

4 tbsp. dry white wine

1 recipe quantity Velouté Sauce
(see page 14)

salt and freshly ground black pepper

1 Crumble the saffron strands into a small bowl, add 2 tablespoons hot water, and leave to soak 15 minutes.

2 Melt 1 tablespoon of the butter in a saucepan, add the shallots and fry genly 5 minutes, or until soft. Add the wine and let bubble slowly until the liquid reduces to about 1 tablespoon.

3 Add the saffron and the soaking liquid to the pan and whisk in the Velouté Sauce. Heat slowly until boiling, stirring, then simmer 10 minutes, stirring occasionally.

4 Remove the pan from the heat and season to taste with salt and pepper. Gradually whisk in the remaining butter until well blended. Serve hot.

SERVING SUGGESTIONS Serve with broiled or poached haddock fillets or monkfish tail.

013 Quick Chili Sauce

PREPARATION TIME 10 minutes   COOKING TIME 20 minutes   SERVES 6

1 tbsp. olive oil or chili-flavored olive oil
5 scallions, finely chopped
1 red chili, seeded and finely chopped
1 garlic clove, crushed
1 can (15-oz.) crushed tomatoes
a squeeze of fresh lemon juice

1 tbsp. light soft brown sugar
2 tsp. cornstarch
bottled medium-hot chili sauce,
   to taste (optional)
salt and freshly ground black pepper

1 Heat the oil in a small saucepan, add the scallions, chili, and garlic and fry 5 minutes, or until soft, stirring occasionally.

2 Add the tomatoes, lemon juice, sugar, and salt and pepper to taste and mix well. Bring slowly to a boil, then cover, lower the heat, and simmer 10 minutes, stirring occasionally.

3 Put the cornstarch and 1 tablespoon cold water in a small bowl and blend until smooth, then stir the cornstarch mixture into the sauce. Bring the sauce to a boil, stirring continuously, then lower the heat and simmer 3 minutes, stirring.

4 Taste and add more salt and pepper, if desired, then add a dash or two of chili sauce, if using. Serve hot.

SERVING SUGGESTIONS Serve with broiled or pan-fried monkfish, halibut, or shrimp. Alternatively, serve with stuffed baked zucchini or bell peppers.

014 Red Wine Sauce

PREPARATION TIME 10 minutes   **COOKING TIME** 15 minutes   **SERVES** 4 to 6

2 tbsp. butter

2 or 3 shallots, finely chopped

1 small garlic clove, crushed

2 tbsp. all-purpose flour

2 tsp. light soft brown sugar

1¼ cups full-bodied red wine

1 tbsp. medium-dry sherry

1 tsp. chopped thyme or rosemary

salt and freshly ground black pepper

1 Melt the butter in a small saucepan, add the shallots and garlic, and fry gently 10 minutes, or or until soft stirring occasionally.

2 Stir in the flour and sugar and cook 1 minute, stirring. Remove the pan from the heat and gradually stir or whisk in the wine and sherry.

3 Return the pan to the heat and bring slowly to a boil, stirring or whisking continuously until the sauce is thicker. Lower the heat and leave to simmer 2 to 3 minutes, stirring.

4 Stir in the thyme and season to taste with salt and pepper. Serve hot.

SERVING SUGGESTIONS Serve with roast beef or broiled pork chops.
COOK'S TIP Choose a red wine with a fairly robust flavor. Once the sauce has been cooked, let it cool slightly, then puree in a blender or food processor until smooth, if desired. Reheat slowly before serving.

015 Mayonnaise

PREPARATION TIME 10 minutes, plus optional chilling   **SERVES** 6 to 8

2 egg yolks
1 tsp. Dijon mustard
1 tbsp. freshly squeezed lemon juice
   or white-wine vinegar

pinch of sugar
1½ cups light olive oil or sunflower oil
salt and freshly ground black pepper

1 Put the egg yolks, mustard, lemon juice, sugar, a little salt and pepper, and 1 tablespoon of the
   oil in a small blender or food processor. Blend 20 seconds, or until smooth, pale, and creamy.
2 With the motor running and the blades turning, gradually add the remaining oil to the blender
   or food processor, pouring it through the feed tube in a slow, continuous stream until the
   mayonnaise is thick, creamy, and smooth.
3 Adjust the seasoning to taste, then use immediately or cover and chill until required. Store in
   a covered container in the refrigerator up to 3 days. Remove the mayonnaise from the
   refrigerator 30 minutes before serving. Serve at room temperature.

SERVING SUGGESTIONS Serve with salads, sliced cold meats, or smoked fish, or use as the basis for
sauces such as Tartare Sauce or flavored mayonnaises.
VARIATION Use fresh lime juice in place of lemon juice or white-wine vinegar.
COOK'S TIP The ingredients for mayonnaise should all be at room temperature. If eggs are used straight from
the refrigerator, the mayonnaise might separate.

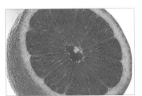

016 Aïoli

PREPARATION TIME 10 minutes, plus optional chilling   SERVES 6 to 8

2 egg yolks
1 tbsp. freshly squeezed lemon juice
4 garlic cloves, crushed

½ tsp. salt
1¼ cups light olive oil or sunflower oil
freshly ground black pepper

1 Put the egg yolks, lemon juice, garlic, salt, a little black pepper and 1 tablespoon of the oil
  in a small blender or food processor. Blend 20 seconds, or until pale and creamy.
2 With the motor running and the blades turning, gradually add the remaining oil to the blender
  or food processor, pouring it through the feed tube in a slow, continuous stream until the aïoli
  is thick, creamy, and smooth.
3 Adjust the seasoning to taste, then use immediately or cover and chill until required. Store
  in a covered container in the refrigerator up to 2 days. Serve cold or leave at room temperature
  30 minutes before serving.

SERVING SUGGESTIONS Serve with cold, sliced roast chicken or salmon fillets, jumbo shrimp, or with
Mediterranean-style fish soups. Alternatively, serve with hard-boiled eggs or as a dip for potato wedges,
potato chips, or vegetable crudités.
VARIATIONS Use fresh lime juice in place of lemon juice. Use smoked garlic in place of standard garlic.
COOK'S TIPS When buying garlic, choose plump garlic bulbs with tightly packed cloves and dry skin. Avoid
bulbs with soft, shriveled cloves or green shoots.
  When using a garlic press, leave the peel on the garlic clove. The soft garlic flesh will be pressed through
the mesh, and the peel/skin will be left behind in the garlic press, making it easy to clean out after use.

017 Herby Lemon Hollandaise

PREPARATION TIME 20 minutes   **COOKING TIME** 2 to 3 minutes   **SERVES** 4 to 6

3 tbsp. white-wine vinegar

6 black peppercorns

1 slice onion or ½ shallot

1 bay leaf

1 blade of mace

2 egg yolks

1 stick butter, at room temperature, diced

1 tbsp. chopped mixed herbs, such as
   parsley, chives, and chervil

freshly squeezed lemon juice, to taste

salt and freshly ground black pepper

1 Put the vinegar in a heavy-bottomed saucepan with the peppercorns, onion, bay leaf, and
   mace. Bring to a boil, then lower the heat and simmer until the mixture reduces to about
   1 tablespoon liquid. Remove from the heat and set aside.

2 Put the egg yolks in a heatproof bowl with 1 tablespoon of the butter and a pinch of salt and
   whisk together. Strain the reduced vinegar into the egg mixture and stir to mix.

3 Put the bowl over a pan of barely simmering water and whisk 3 to 4 minutes, until the mixture
   is pale and begins to thicken.

4 Gradually whisk in the remaining butter, one piece at a time, until the mixture is thicker and
   begins to emulsify. Make sure each piece of butter is incorporated before adding the next piece.

5 Once all the butter has been added and the sauce is light and thick, remove the bowl from the
   heat. Whisk 1 minute. Stir in the herbs, then adjust the seasoning and add a little lemon juice
   to taste. Serve immediately.

SERVING SUGGESTIONS Serve with salmon fillets or whole rainbow trout.

018 Tartar Sauce

PREPARATION TIME 10 minutes, plus standing **SERVES** 8 to 10

4 tbsp. drained and finely chopped
  gherkins
2 tbsp. drained and finely chopped
  capers
1 cup Mayonnaise (see page 25)
4 tbsp. lightly whipped heavy cream

1 tbsp. tarragon vinegar
1 tbsp. chopped flat-leaf parsley
1 tbsp. snipped chives
2 tsp. chopped tarragon
salt and freshly ground black pepper

1 Put the gherkins, capers, and mayonnaise in a bowl and mix well, then fold in the cream.
2 Fold in the vinegar and herbs and season to taste with salt and pepper.
3 Cover and leave in a cool place at least 30 minutes before serving, to let the flavors develop.
  Serve chilled.

SERVING SUGGESTIONS Serve with broiled or baked fishcakes or fish sticks. Alternatively, serve with fried breadcrumb- or batter-coated cod, flounder, or haddock.
VARIATIONS Use sour cream, crème fraîche, or plain yogurt in place of cream. Use white-wine vinegar or freshly squeezed lemon juice in place of tarragon vinegar.
COOK'S TIP Capers are the small, unopened buds of a thorny, wild Mediterranean plant, which are picked and then pickled in salty vinegar or preserved in salt. Capers should be rinsed (if preserved in salt) and drained before use. They can be used whole or finely chopped, depending on the recipe.

019 Red Currant & Cranberry Sauce

PREPARATION TIME 5 minutes, plus cooling   **COOKING TIME** 25 minutes   **SERVES** 4

⅓ cup red currant jelly

1 cup cranberries

juice and finely grated zest of 1 orange

1 cinnamon stick

2 tbsp. ruby port

1 Put the red currant jelly in a saucepan, add the cranberries, orange juice and zest, cinnamon stick and port and stir to mix.

2 Bring slowly to a boil, stirring, then simmer, uncovered, about 20 minutes, or until the cranberries are soft and the sauce thickens slightly, stirring frequently.

3 Serve warm or cold. If serving cold, remove the pan from the heat and set aside until cold. Remove and discard the cinnamon stick before serving.

SERVING SUGGESTIONS Serve with broiled or pan-fried beef steaks, or with roast turkey, venison, or pheasant.

VARIATION Use blueberries in place of cranberries.

COOK'S TIP Frozen cranberries can also be used for this recipe. If you are using frozen cranberries, they can be used frozen (preferable) or defrosted—you might also need to reduce the overall cooking time a little.

020 Cranberry & Orange Sauce

PREPARATION TIME 5 minutes, plus optional cooling   **COOKING TIME** 30 minutes
SERVES 6 to 8

2 cups cranberries

juice and finely grated zest of 1 small orange

scant ½ cup sugar

1–2 tbsp. ruby port (optional)

1 Put the cranberries in a saucepan with the orange juice, sugar, and ⅔ cup water.

2 Bring slowly to a boil, then cook, uncovered, 20 to 30 minutes, or until the cranberries are soft, stirring occasionally.

3 Remove the pan from the heat and let cool slightly. Using a slotted spoon, remove half the cranberries and place in a bowl. Puree the remainder and juice in a blender or food processor.

4 Add the cranberry puree to the reserved cranberries in the bowl, then stir in the orange zest and port, if using, mixing well. Serve warm or cold.

SERVING SUGGESTIONS Serve with hot or cold roast turkey, chicken, pork, or duck.
COOK'S TIP Cranberries are in season and at their peak from late fall into the winter months. You can also purchase them frozen all year round.

021 Classic Pesto

PREPARATION TIME 10 minutes   **SERVES** 4 to 6

2½ cups basil leaves, roughly torn
   into pieces
½ cup pine nuts
1 garlic clove, crushed

7 tbsp. extra-virgin olive oil
½ cup freshly grated Parmesan cheese
salt and freshly ground black pepper

1 Put the basil in a mortar with the pine nuts, garlic, and a little of the oil. Pound or grind with
  a pestle to make a paste. Gradually work in the remaining oil, then stir in the Parmesan and
  season to taste with salt and pepper.

2 Alternatively, put the basil, pine nuts, garlic, and olive oil in a small blender or food processor
  and blend to form a fairly smooth paste. Add the Parmesan and salt and pepper to taste and
  process again briefly to mix.

3 Store the pesto in a screw-topped jar, covered with a thin layer of oil, in the refrigerator for
  up to 1 week. Serve cold.

SERVING SUGGESTIONS Serve with hot gnocchi or linguine. Alternatively, serve with grilled or roast chicken
portions or haddock or cod steak.
VARIATION Use 1¼ cups parsley in place of 1¼ cups of the basil.

022 Satay Sauce

PREPARATION TIME 10 minutes   **COOKING TIME** 25 minutes   **SERVES** 6 to 8

¾ cup dry roasted or unsalted (toasted) peanuts

1 tbsp. olive oil

3 shallots, finely chopped

2 garlic cloves, crushed

1 red or green chili, seeded and finely chopped

1-inch piece gingerroot, peeled and finely chopped

scant 1 cup coconut milk

juice of 1 lime

1 tbsp. light soft brown sugar

salt

1 Put the peanuts in a blender or food processor and process until they are finely chopped. Set aside.

2 Heat the oil in a saucepan, add the shallots and fry gently 5 minutes, or until soft. Add the garlic, chili, and ginger and fry 2 minutes longer, stirring occasionally.

3 Remove the pan from the heat, then add the shallot mixture to the peanuts in the processor and process briefly to mix.

4 Return the mixture to the pan, then stir in the coconut milk, lime juice, and sugar.

5 Bring slowly to a boil, stirring, then lower the heat and simmer, uncovered, 10 to 15 minutes, or until the sauce is thick, stirring occasionally. Season with salt, if required. Serve hot.

SERVING SUGGESTIONS Serve as a dipping sauce with marinated grilled or barbecued beef or chicken kabobs. Alternatively, serve with a selection of cooked vegetables or vegetable crudités.

Chapter 2

SAUCES FOR PASTA

Pasta comes in a vast array of shapes and sizes and it cries out for the addition of a delicious, homemade sauce. Pasta sauces should be served with freshly cooked, hot pasta, either on top of the pasta or tossed lightly together with the pasta. Serving suggestions are included with each recipe, recommending a specific pasta shape. There are not hard and fast rules for saucing pasta, however, so treat these these ideas as exactly that and use the shapes you have.

A wide selection of authentic and more contemporary pasta sauces are included. Choose from Garlic & Chili Sauce, Spicy Tomato Sauce, Hazelnut Pesto Sauce, Chorizo & Plum Tomato Sauce, Zucchini & Mixed Pepper Sauce, Spinach & Blue Cheese Sauce, Cajun Chicken Sauce, or Creamy Smoked Salmon Sauce, as well as more traditional favorites such as Fresh Tomato & Basil Sauce, Bolognese Sauce, Primavera or Carbonara.

Zucchini & Mixed Pepper Sauce (see page 39)

023 **Primavera Sauce**

PREPARATION TIME 15 minutes   **COOKING TIME** 25 minutes   **SERVES** 4

2 carrots, finely diced
2 zucchini, sliced
2 cups small broccoli florets
¾ cup asparagus cut into 1-inch pieces
1 cup frozen peas
1 bunch scallions, chopped
1 garlic clove, crushed

1 can (15-oz.) crushed tomatoes
⅔ cup vegetable stock (homemade or from
   a bouillon cube)
1 tbsp. chopped parsley
1 tbsp. chopped basil
salt and freshly ground black pepper

1 Put the carrots, zucchini, broccoli, asparagus, peas, scallions, garlic, tomatoes, and stock in
   a saucepan, season with salt and pepper, and bring slowly to a boil, stirring occasionally. Lower
   the heat, cover, and simmer 10 minutes, stirring from time to time.
2 Uncover the pan, increase the heat slightly, and cook 5 to 10 minutes longer until the
   vegetables are cooked and tender, stirring occasionally.
3 Stir in the herbs and season again to taste with salt and pepper. Serve hot.

SERVING SUGGESTIONS Serve with hot pasta, such as fusilli, spirali, or riccioli. Sprinkle with freshly grated
Parmesan cheese just before serving, if desired.
VARIATION Use sugar-snap peas or frozen fava beans in place of peas.

024 Garlic & Chili Sauce

PREPARATION TIME 10 minutes   **COOKING TIME** 10 minutes   **SERVES** 4

5 tbsp. olive oil

1 small onion, finely chopped

3 to 4 garlic cloves, finely chopped
or crushed

2 small red chilies, finely chopped
(for a milder flavor, remove and
discard the seeds)

4 sun-dried tomatoes in oil, drained, patted
dry, and finely chopped

2 to 3 tbsp. chopped parsley or basil

salt and freshly ground black pepper

1 Heat 1 tablespoon of the oil in a saucepan, add the onion, garlic, and chilies and fry about
5 minutes, or until soft.

2 Add the remaining oil to the pan together with the sun-dried tomatoes. Heat slowly until hot,
stirring continuously.

3 Stir in the herbs and season to taste with salt and pepper. Serve hot.

SERVING SUGGESTIONS Serve with hot pasta, such as spaghetti, spaghettini, or tagliatelle. Sprinkle the
tossed pasta with a generous amount of freshly grated Parmesan cheese just before serving.

VARIATIONS Use green chilies in place of red chilies. Use ¼ to ⅓ cup chopped or sliced pitted black olives
in place of sun-dried tomatoes.

025 Fresh Tomato & Basil Sauce

PREPARATION TIME 15 minutes   **COOKING TIME** 35 minutes   **SERVES** 4

1 tbsp. olive oil

6 shallots, finely chopped

2 garlic cloves, finely chopped

2 celery sticks, finely chopped

3¾ cups skinned, seeded, and chopped
tomatoes

4 sun-dried tomatoes in oil, drained, patted
dry, and finely chopped

2 tbsp. medium-dry sherry

1 tbsp. tomato paste

½ tsp. light soft brown sugar

2 to 3 tbsp. chopped basil

salt and freshly ground black pepper

1 Heat the oil in a saucepan, add the shallots, garlic, and celery and fry 5 minutes, or until soft,
stirring occasionally.

2 Add the tomatoes, sun-dried tomatoes, sherry, tomato paste, sugar, and salt and pepper
to taste, and mix well. Bring to a boil, then lower the heat, cover, and simmer 15 minutes,
stirring occasionally.

3 Uncover the pan, increase the heat slightly, and cook 10 to 15 minutes longer, until the sauce
is cooked and thick, stirring occasionally. Stir in the basil. Serve hot.

SERVING SUGGESTIONS Serve with hot pasta, such as penne or fusilli. Sprinkle with freshly grated
Parmesan cheese and garnish with basil sprigs. This sauce is also delicious served with hot filled pasta,
such as tortelloni or ravioli.
VARIATIONS Use 1 or 2 leeks in place of shallots. Use 2 small carrots in place of celery. Use chopped
mixed herbs in place of basil.

026 Zucchini & Mixed Pepper Sauce

PREPARATION TIME 10 minutes   COOKING TIME 30 minutes   SERVES 4

4 tbsp. butter

1 red onion, finely chopped

1 garlic clove, crushed

1 red bell pepper, halved, seeded, and diced

1 yellow bell pepper, halved, seeded, and diced

4 zucchini, sliced

2 cups sliced button mushrooms

1 can (15-oz.) crushed tomatoes

⅔ cup dried-red red wine

1 tbsp. tomato paste

2 tbsp. chopped basil

salt and freshly ground black pepper

1 Melt the butter in a saucepan, add the onion, garlic, red and yellow peppers, and zucchini and fry 5 minutes, or until slightly soft. Add the mushrooms, tomatoes, red wine, and tomato paste, season to taste with salt and pepper, and stir to mix. Bring to a boil, then lower the heat, cover, and simmer 10 minutes, stirring occasionally.

2 Uncover the pan, increase the heat a little, and cook 10 to 15 minutes longer, or until the sauce is slightly thicker and the vegetables are tender, stirring occasionally. Stir in the basil and adjust the seasoning to taste. Serve hot.

SERVING SUGGESTIONS Serve with hot pasta, such as spaghetti or fettuccine.
VARIATIONS Use 1 standard onion or 4 shallots in place of red onion. Use dry white wine or vegetable stock in place of red wine.

027 Hazelnut Pesto Sauce

PREPARATION TIME 10 minutes, plus optional chilling   **SERVES** 4

2½ cups basil leaves, roughly torn into
   pieces
½ cup blanched hazelnuts, lightly toasted
2 garlic cloves, crushed

7 tbsp. olive oil
¾ cup freshly grated Parmesan cheese
salt and freshly ground black pepper

1 Put the basil, hazelnuts, garlic, and olive oil in a small blender or food processor and blend
   until fairly smooth and thoroughly mixed. Add the Parmesan and salt and pepper to taste and
   blend again briefly to mix.

2 Alternatively, put the basil in a mortar with the hazelnuts, garlic, and a little of the oil. Pound
   or grind with a pestle to make a paste. Gradually work in the remaining oil, then stir in the
   Parmesan and season to taste with salt and pepper.

3 Transfer to a small bowl, cover, and set aside until ready to serve. Alternatively, store the pesto
   in a screw-topped jar, covered with a thin layer of oil, in the refrigerator up to 1 week.
   Serve cold.

SERVING SUGGESTIONS Serve with hot filled pasta, such as ravioli. Alternatively, serve with hot pasta,
such as plain spaghetti, spinach tagliatelle, farfalle, or fusilli.
VARIATION Use lightly toasted walnuts or almonds instead of hazelnuts.
COOK'S TIP Basil is a delicate herb that should be prepared carefully. To avoid losing flavor and color too
quickly, tear the leaves with your fingers instead of chopping with a knife just before using.

028 Spinach & Blue Cheese Sauce

PREPARATION TIME 15 minutes   **COOKING TIME** 15 minutes   **SERVES** 4

2 tbsp. butter

4 shallots, finely chopped

1 garlic clove, crushed

3 tbsp. all-purpose flour

2 cups milk

12 oz. spinach, cooked and
    thoroughly drained

4 oz. Stilton or other blue cheese,
    crumbled

salt and freshly ground black pepper

1 Melt the butter in a saucepan, add the shallots and garlic, and fry gently 5 minutes, or until soft. Add the flour and cook for 1 minute, stirring.

2 Remove the pan from the heat and gradually stir or whisk in the milk. Return the pan to the heat and cook slowly, stirring or whisking continuously until the sauce comes to a boil and becomes thicker. Simmer 2 to 3 minutes, stirring.

3 Press any excess water out of the spinach using the back of a wooden spoon, then chop the spinach. Add the spinach and Stilton to the sauce and mix well.

4 Reheat slowly, stirring continuously, until the cheese melts and the sauce is hot. Season to taste with salt and pepper. Serve hot.

SERVING SUGGESTIONS Serve with hot pasta, such as tagliatelle, linguine, or spaghetti.
VARIATIONS Use 1 onion in place of shallots. Use diced Gorgonzola, diced Cambozola/blue Brie, or grated sharp Cheddar in place of Stilton.
COOK'S TIP Other quick-and-easy ways to squeeze excess water out of the spinach are to tip the cooked spinach into a colander and press with a potato masher, or press between two plates.

029 **Tasty Tuna Sauce**

PREPARATION TIME 10 minutes   **COOKING TIME** 15 minutes   **SERVES** 4

4 tbsp. butter

2½ cups trimmed, washed, and sliced
leeks

3¼ cups sliced button mushrooms

3 tbsp all-purpose flour

2 cups milk

14 oz. canned tuna in spring water, brine,
or oil, drained and flaked

2 to 3 tbsp. chopped parsley

a good pinch cayenne pepper

salt and freshly ground black pepper

1 Melt the butter in a saucepan, add the leeks and mushrooms, and fry gently 10 minutes,
or until soft, stirring occasionally. Add the flour and cook slowly 1 minute, stirring.

2 Remove the pan from the heat and gradually stir or whisk in the milk, then heat slowly,
stirring or whisking continuously until the sauce comes to a boil and becomes thicker. Simmer
2 to 3 minutes, stirring.

3 Stir in the tuna, parsley, cayenne pepper, and salt and pepper to taste, then reheat slowly until
hot, stirring. Serve hot.

SERVING SUGGESTIONS Serve with hot pasta, such as spaghetti, tagliatelle, linguine, or angle hair pasta.
VARIATIONS Use flaked canned salmon in place of tuna. Use sliced zucchini in place of mushrooms. Use
1 tablespoon chopped tarragon or cilantro in place of parsley.

030 Creamy Smoked Salmon Sauce

PREPARATION TIME 10 minutes   **COOKING TIME** 15 minutes   **SERVES** 4

2 tbsp. butter

4 cups button mushrooms, halved

⅔ cup dry white wine

1¼ cups crème fraîche

10 oz. smoked salmon, cut into thin strips
  or small pieces

1 tbsp. chopped dill

1 tbsp. creamed horseradish sauce

salt and freshly ground black pepper

1 Melt the butter in a saucepan, add the mushrooms, and fry 5 minutes, or until soft.

2 Add the wine and bring to a boil, then cook over high heat until the liquid reduces by half,
   stirring occasionally.

3 Lower the heat, stir in the crème fraîche, and simmer.

4 Stir in the smoked salmon, dill, creamed horseradish sauce, and salt and pepper to taste, and
   heat slowly 1 to 2 minutes, stirring. Serve hot.

SERVING SUGGESTIONS Serve with hot pasta, such as linguine, spaghetti, fettuccine, or tagliatelle.
VARIATIONS Use sliced zucchini in place of mushrooms. Use heavy cream or sour cream in place of crème
fraîche. Use chopped flat-leaf parsley or snipped chives in place of dill.
COOK'S TIP You can buy smoked salmon trimmings, which are ideal to use in this recipe, and these will be
more economical, too.

031 Red Salmon & Watercress Sauce

PREPARATION TIME 10 minutes   COOKING TIME 15 minutes   SERVES 4

4 tsp. butter
3 shallots, finely chopped
1 garlic clove, crushed
6 oz. watercress, washed and patted dry

1¼ cups crème fraîche
1 tsp. Dijon mustard
14 oz. canned red salmon in brine, drained
salt and freshly ground black pepper

1 Melt the butter in a saucepan, add the shallots, garlic, and watercress, and fry 5 minutes, until the shallots are soft.
2 Remove the pan from the heat and set aside to cool slightly, then place the watercress mixture in a blender or food processor. Add the crème fraîche, mustard, and salt and pepper to taste and blend until smooth.
3 Transfer the mixture to a saucepan and heat slowly until hot, stirring continuously.
4 Flake the salmon, removing any bones, then add the salmon to the sauce. Reheat slowly until hot, stirring continuously. Adjust the seasoning to taste and serve hot.

SERVING SUGGESTIONS Serve with hot pasta, such as farfalle, conchiglie, or penne.
VARIATIONS Use 1 small standard onion or red onion in place of shallots. Use flaked canned pink salmon or tuna in place of red salmon.

032 Cajun Chicken Sauce

PREPARATION TIME 15 minutes   COOKING TIME 15 minutes   SERVES 4

1 tbsp. olive oil

1 onion, finely chopped

1 red belll pepper, halved, seeded,
   and sliced

2 small zucchini, cut into matchstick strips

4 cups button mushrooms, halved

1 lb. skinless, boneless chicken breast
   halves, cut into thin strips

1 tbsp. Cajun seasoning

1 tbsp. cornstarch

2 tbsp. dry sherry

1¼ cups chicken stock (homemade
   or from a bouillon cube)

2 tbsp. tomato paste

salt and freshly ground black pepper

1 Heat the oil in a wok or large skillet, add the onion, red pepper, zucchini, and mushrooms and
   stir-fry 3 minutes.

2 Add the chicken and stir-fry 3 to 4 minutes, until the chicken is cooked through. Add the Cajun
   seasoning and stir-fry 1 minute longer.

3 Blend the cornstarch with the sherry until smooth and add to the wok with the stock, tomato
   paste, and salt and pepper to taste. Stir-fry until hot and bubbling, then simmer 2 to 3 minutes,
   stirring continuously. Serve hot.

SERVING SUGGESTIONS Serve with hot pasta, such as tagliatelle, fettuccine, or spaghetti.
VARIATIONS Use carrots in place of zucchini. Use turkey breast or pork tenderloin in place of chicken.

033 Chicken, Leek & Mushroom Sauce

PREPARATION TIME 15 minutes   **COOKING TIME** 20 minutes   **SERVES** 4 to 6

3 tbsp. butter

2 leeks, washed and thinly sliced

4 cups sliced mushrooms

1/3 cup all-purpose flour

1¼ cups milk

2/3 cup chicken stock (homemade or from
   a bouillon cube), cool

12 oz. cooked skinless, boneless chicken,
   cut into small pieces

1 to 2 tbsp. chopped parsley

salt and freshly ground black pepper

1 Melt the butter in a saucepan, add the leeks and mushrooms, and fry gently 10 minutes,
   or until soft.
2 Add the flour and cook 1 minute, stirring. Remove the pan from the heat and gradually stir
   or whisk in the milk and stock.
3 Return the pan to the heat and cook slowly, stirring continuously, until the sauce comes
   to a boil and becomes thicker. Lower the heat and simmer 2 to 3 minutes longer, stirring.
4 Add the chicken to the sauce and bring back to a boil, stirring continuously, then simmer
   5 minutes longer, stirring occasionally.
5 Stir in the parsley and season to taste with salt and pepper. Serve hot.

SERVING SUGGESTIONS Serve with hot pasta, such as fusilli or riccioli.
VARIATIONS Use cooked turkey breast or cooked ham in place of chicken. Use 1 tablespoon chopped
tarragon, cilantro, or mixed herbs in place of parsley.

034 Chorizo & Plum Tomato Sauce

PREPARATION TIME 20 minutes   COOKING TIME 30 minutes   SERVES 4

4 tbsp. butter

1 red onion, finely chopped

1 small red bell pepper, halved, seeded, and finely chopped

2 celery sticks, finely chopped

2 garlic cloves, crushed

6 oz. chorizo sausage, thinly sliced

1 can (15-oz.) crushed tomatoes

4 sun-dried tomatoes in oil, drained, patted dry, and finely chopped

6 tbsp. dry white wine

1 tbsp. sun-dried tomato paste

2 to 3 tbsp. chopped basil

salt and freshly ground black pepper

1 Melt the butter in a saucepan, add the onion, red pepper, celery, and garlic and fry 5 minutes. Add the chorizo and fry 1 minute longer.

2 Add the canned tomatoes, sun-dried tomatoes, white wine, tomato paste, and salt and pepper to taste, and stir to mix, breaking up the tomatoes with the spoon. Bring to a boil, then lower the heat, cover, and simmer 15 minutes, stirring occasionally.

3 Uncover the pan, increase the heat slightly, and cook 5 to 10 minutes longer, or until the sauce is cooked and slightly thicker, stirring occasionally. Stir in the basil. Serve hot.

SERVING SUGGESTIONS Serve with hot pasta, such as tagliatelle or fettuccine.
VARIATIONS Use fresh tomatoes in place of canned tomatoes—peeled and chop 18 oz. ripe plum or vine-ripened tomatoes and use as directed. Use red wine in place of white wine.

035 **Carbonara Sauce**

PREPARATION TIME 10 minutes   **COOKING TIME** 15 minutes   **SERVES** 4

12 oz. dried spaghetti

2 tbsp. butter

1 tbsp. olive oil

1 onion, finely chopped

1 cup chopped thick bacon

3 eggs, beaten

6 tbsp. heavy cream

$\frac{1}{3}$ cup freshly grated pecorino cheese

$\frac{3}{4}$ cup freshly grated Parmesan cheese

2 tbsp. chopped parsley or snipped chives

salt and freshly ground black pepper

1 Cook the spaghetti in a large saucepan of lightly salted, boiling water 10 to 12 minutes, until just cooked or al dente.

2 Meanwhile, melt the butter with the oil in another pan. Add the onion and fry about 5 minutes, until the onion is soft.

3 Add the bacon and cook 5 minutes longer, or until the bacon is cooked, stirring frequently. Remove the pan from the heat and set aside.

4 Mix the eggs, cream, pecorino, two-thirds of the Parmesan, the parsley, and salt and pepper, to taste together in a bowl.

5 Drain the pasta and return it to the rinsed-out pan. Add the bacon mixture and toss to mix. Add the egg mixture and cook slowly over very low heat, tossing continuously, until the eggs are just lightly cooked. Sprinkle with the remaining Parmesan and serve immediately.

SERVING SUGGESTIONS Serve with other hot pasta, such as tagliatelle, instead of spaghetti.
VARIATION Use smoked pancetta, with the rind removed, in place of bacon.

036 Bolognese Sauce

PREPARATION TIME 10 minutes   **COOKING TIME** 1 hour 10 minutes   **SERVES** 4 to 6

1 tbsp. olive oil
2 red onions, chopped
1 carrot, finely chopped
2 celery sticks, finely chopped
1 garlic clove, crushed
1 lb. 2 oz. lean ground beef
1 tbsp. all-purpose flour
4 cups sliced mushrooms

1 can (15-oz.) crushed tomatoes
1 tbsp. tomato paste
1¼ cups beef or vegetable stock
   (homemade or from a bouillon cube)
1¼ cups dry red or white wine
2 tsp. dried Italian herbs
salt and freshly ground black pepper

1 Heat the oil in a large saucepan, add the onions, carrot, celery, and garlic and fry 5 minutes, or until the vegetables are soft.

2 Add the ground beef and cook until the meat is brown all over, stirring occasionally. Add the flour and cook 1 minute, stirring.

3 Add the mushrooms, tomatoes, tomato paste, stock, wine, dried herbs, and salt and pepper to taste and stir to mix, breaking up the tomatoes with the spoon.

4 Bring to a boil, then lower the heat, cover, and simmer about 1 hour, stirring occasionally, until the meat is cooked and the sauce reduces. If desired, uncover the pan and increase the heat slightly 15 to 20 minutes before the end of the cooking time to thicken the sauce a little more. Serve hot.

SERVING SUGGESTIONS Serve with hot pasta, such as spaghetti or linguini. Serve sprinkled with freshly grated Parmesan cheese.
VARIATIONS Use lean ground pork or lamb in place of beef. Use extra stock in place of red wine.

Chapter 3

SAUCES FOR MEAT & FISH

Freshly broiled, grilled, or pan-fried meat, poultry, or game served with a simple, tasty sauce is a combination that's difficult to beat. In the following pages you'll find a wide variety of appetizing sauces, with something suitable for all occasions.

These sauces are quick and easy to make and will add a delicious finishing touch to any meal. Choose from classics, such as Lemon Caper Sauce or Madeira Sauce, or try something a little less conventional like Plum & Ginger Sauce or Spiced Green Lentil Sauce.

Most fish and shellfish are best simply broiled, baked, or pan-fried, and then served with a delicious sauce, such as Marie Rose Sauce, Cheese & Chive Sauce, Dill & Mustard Sauce, Wild Mushroom Sauce, Creamy Fresh Lemon Sauce, and Herb & Lime Butter.

Lemon-Caper Sauce (see page 65)

037 **Wild Mushroom Sauce**

PREPARATION TIME 10 minutes   **COOKING TIME** 15 minutes   **SERVES** 4

2 tbsp. butter

2 shallots, thinly sliced

1 garlic clove, crushed

5 cups sliced mixed wild mushrooms, such
  as shiitake and oyster mushrooms

2 tbsp. dry sherry

2 to 3 tsp. chopped thyme (optional)

2 to 3 tbsp. crème fraîche or sour cream

salt and freshly ground black pepper

1 Melt the butter in a large, nonstick skillet. Add the shallots and garlic and fry gently
  3 minutes.

2 Add the mushrooms and fry 5 minutes, or until tender.

3 Stir in the sherry and thyme, if using, increase the heat slightly, and cook 2 to 3 minutes, until
  most of the liquid evaporates, stirring continously.

4 Stir in the crème fraîche and season to taste with salt and pepper. Serve hot.

SERVING SUGGESTIONS Serve with broiled or pan-fried halibut or salmon steaks, or with broiled or oven-
baked whole trout or mackerel.

VARIATIONS Use button or cremini mushrooms (or a mixture) in place of wild mushrooms. Use brandy, ruby
port, or Madeira in place of sherry. Use chopped sage or tarragon in place of thyme. Use 1 to 2 tablespoons
chopped parsley in place of thyme.

038 Dill & Mustard Sauce

PREPARATION TIME 5 minutes **COOKING TIME** 20 minutes **SERVES** 6

¾ cup dry white wine
¾ cup fish or vegetable stock (homemade or from a bouillon cube)
¾ cup crème fraîche or sour cream

2 tbsp. wholegrain mustard
2 egg yolks, lightly beaten
2 to 3 tbsp. chopped dill
salt and freshly ground black pepper

1 Put the wine and stock in a saucepan and bring to a boil, then boil rapidly until the liquid reduces by about half.

2 Lower the heat and stir in the crème fraîche, mustard, egg yolks, and dill.

3 Cook slowly, stirring continuously, about 10 minutes, until the sauce thickens slightly. Do not let the sauce boil. Season to taste with salt and pepper. Serve hot.

SERVING SUGGESTIONS Serve with pan-fried or broiled flounder, perch, lemon sole, or halibut fillets, or with pan-fried or barbecued shrimp.

VARIATIONS Use 1 to 2 tablespoons Dijon mustard in place of wholegrain mustard. Use 1 to 2 tablespoons chopped tarragon or 2 to 3 teaspoons horseradish sauce (or to taste) in place of dill.

COOK'S TIPS Egg yolks are added to sauces such as this one toward the end of the cooking time. They will enrich and thicken a sauce, but remember the eggs will curdle if the mixture is boiled.

Once made, this sauce should be served immediately as it cannot be reheated.

039 Sage & Red Onion Sauce

PREPARATION TIME 10 minutes   **COOKING TIME** 15 minutes   **SERVES** 4 to 6

4 tbsp. butter

2 red onions, finely chopped

3 tbsp. all-purpose flour

⅔ cup milk

⅔ cup vegetable stock (homemade or from
a bouillon cube), cool

a squeeze of fresh lime juice
(optional)

1 to 2 tbsp. chopped sage

salt and freshly ground black pepper

1 Melt half of the butter in a skillet, add the onions and fry gently for 10 minutes, or until soft.
Remove the pan from the heat, set aside, and keep hot.

2 Meanwhile, put the remaining butter in a saucepan with the flour, milk, stock, and lime juice, if
using. Heat slowly, whisking continuously, until the sauce comes to a boil and thickens. Lower
the heat and simmer 3 to 4 minutes, stirring.

3 Stir in the fried onions and sage and reheat slowly until hot, stirring continuously. Season to
taste with salt and pepper. Serve hot.

SERVING SUGGESTIONS Serve with pan-fried or roast chicken, duck, pheasant, or rabbit.
VARIATION Use yellow onions in place of red onions.

040 **Horseradish Butter**

PREPARATION TIME 10 minutes, plus chilling SERVES 4 to 6

1 stick (½ cup) unsalted butter,
   at room temperature
1½ tbsp. horseradish sauce

2 tbsp. finely snipped chives
freshly ground black pepper

1 Put the butter in a small bowl and beat until soft. Add the horseradish sauce, snipped chives, and black pepper to taste, and beat until well mixed.
2 Put the flavored butter onto a piece of plastic wrap and shape into a log. Wrap the butter in the plastic warp, then chill in the refrigerator at least 1 hour before serving. Cut into 4 to 6 even slices to serve. Serve chilled.

SERVING SUGGESTIONS Serve a slice of flavored butter on top of broiled or pan-fried beef or venison steaks, pork chops, or roasted pieces of turkey breast.

041 **Chili Sauce**

PREPARATION TIME 10 minutes   **COOKING TIME** 20 minutes   **SERVES** 4 to 6

1 can (15-oz.) crushed tomatoes

2 shallots, finely chopped

2 celery sticks, finely chopped

1 red chili, seeded and finely chopped

1 garlic clove, crushed

⅔ cup dry white wine

1 tbsp. tomato paste

salt and freshly ground black pepper

1 Put the tomatoes, shallots, celery, chili, garlic, wine, tomato paste, and salt and pepper to taste in a small saucepan and stir to mix.

2 Bring the tomato mixture to a boil. Lower the heat to medium-low and cook, uncovered, 15 to 20 minutes, until the sauce is cooked and thick, stirring occasionally. Adjust the seasoning to taste and serve hot.

SERVING SUGGESTIONS Serve with stir-fried jumbo shrimp tossed with cooked rice noodles. Alternatively, serve with broiled or oven-baked whole sardines or mackerel.

VARIATIONS Use red wine or unsweetened apple juice in place of white wine. Use 1 to 2 teaspoons cayenne pepper, to taste, in place of whole chili. Use 1 poound fresh tomatoes, peeled and chopped, in place of canned tomatoes.

042 Spiced Green Lentil Sauce

PREPARATION TIME 15 minutes   **COOKING TIME** 1 hour 20 minutes **SERVES** 6 to 8

1 tbsp. olive oil

1 onion, finely chopped

1 carrot, finely chopped

2 celery sticks, finely chopped

1 tsp. each ground cumin, ground coriander, ground allspice, and cayenne pepper

1 cup green lentils

2 cups vegetable stock (homemade or from a bouillon cube)

3 tbsp. medium-dry sherry

2 tbsp. chopped flat-leaf parsley

salt and freshly ground black pepper

1 Heat the oil in a saucepan, add the onion, carrot, and celery and fry gently 10 minutes, or until soft.

2 Stir in the ground spices and cook 1 minute, stirring. Add the lentils, stock, sherry, and salt and pepper to taste and mix well.

3 Bring slowly to a boil, then cover and simmer 1 hour, or until the lentils are cooked and soft, stirring occasionally.

4 Stir in the parsley and adjust the seasoning to taste. Serve hot.

SERVING SUGGESTIONS Serve with North African-style barbecued lamb or beef and vegetable kabobs.
COOK'S TIP If you prefer a smoother sauce, once the lentils are cooked and soft, remove the pan from the heat and stir in the chopped parsley. Set aside to cool slightly, then puree briefly in a blender or food processor. Return the sauce to the rinsed-out pan and reheat slowly until hot, stirring.

043 Cheese & Chive Sauce

PREPARATION TIME 5 minutes   COOKING TIME 10 minutes   SERVES 4

1 tbsp. butter

1 tbsp. all-purpose flour

⅔ cup milk

⅔ cup chicken stock (homemade or from
  a bouillon cube), cool

½ cup grated sharp cheddar cheese

2 to 3 tbsp. snipped chives

salt and freshly ground black pepper

1 Put the butter, flour, milk, and stock in a saucepan and heat slowly, whisking continuously, until the sauce comes to a boil and thickens. Lower the heat and simmer 3 to 4 minutes, stirring.

2 Remove the pan from the heat and stir in the cheddar until it melts. Stir in the snipped chives and season to taste with salt and pepper. Serve hot.

SERVING SUGGESTIONS Serve with poached smoked haddock fillets, or with pan-fried cod steaks.
VARIATIONS Use Gruyère or Swiss cheese in place of cheddar. Use chopped parsley in place of chives.

044 **Marie Rose Sauce**

PREPARATION TIME 15 minutes, plus optional chilling   **SERVES** 4 to 6

¾ cup Mayonnaise *(see page 25)*

4 tbsp. lightly whipped heavy cream

2 tbsp. tomato ketchup

1 tsp. Worcestershire sauce

1 tsp. fresh lemon or lime juice

2 tsp. creamed horseradish sauce (optional)

a few drops of hot-pepper sauce

salt and freshly ground black pepper

1 Put the mayonnaise and cream in a bowl and stir until well mixed.

2 Add the tomato ketchup, Worcestershire sauce, lemon juice, creamed horseradish sauce, if using, and hot-pepper sauce and mix well.

3 Season to taste with salt and pepper. Serve immediately or cover and chill until ready to serve. Serve cold.

SERVING SUGGESTIONS Serve with chilled cooked jumbo shrimp, mixed seafood, or flaked crabmeat.
COOK'S TIPS Worcestershire sauce is a strongly flavored proprietary brown sauce/condiment, which is good served with roasted or broiled meat and poultry, or it can be added to recipes such as this one, or to salad dressings and other sauces to heighten the flavor.

Fiery hot-pepper sauce also adds flavor and heat to sauces, marinades, and salad dressings.

045 Creamy Curry Sauce

PREPARATION TIME 10 minutes   **COOKING TIME** 20 minutes   **SERVES** 4 to 6

3 tbsp. butter

1 onion, finely chopped

1 garlic clove, crushed

2 tbsp. all-purpose flour

3 tbsp. medium-hot curry paste

1 tbsp. tomato paste

1 cup + 2 tbsp. vegetable or chicken stock
   (homemade or from a bouillon cube)

¾ cup light cream

salt and freshly ground black pepper

1 Melt the butter in a saucepan, add the onion and fry gently 8 to 10 minutes, until soft and
light brown.

2 Add the garlic and fry 1 minute, then add the flour and cook 1 minute, stirring. Stir in the curry
paste and tomato paste. Remove the pan from the heat and gradually stir or whisk in the stock.

3 Return the pan to the heat and heat slowly, stirring or whisking continuously, until the sauce
comes to a boil and thickens. Simmer 2 to 3 minutes, stirring.

4 Stir in the cream and reheat slowly until hot but not boiling, stirring continuously. Season to
taste with salt and pepper. Serve hot.

SERVING SUGGESTIONS Serve with broiled or pan-fried pork or lamb chops, or chicken thighs.

046 Madeira Sauce

PREPARATION TIME 5 minutes   COOKING TIME 10 minutes   SERVES 4

1 tbsp. olive oil
6 shallots, sliced
4 tbsp. vegetable stock (homemade
   or from a bouillon cube)

4 tbsp. Madeira
1 tsp. dried herbes de Provence
2 tbsp. crème fraîche
salt and freshly ground black pepper

1 Heat the oil in a saucepan, add the shallots, and fry 5 minutes, or until soft.
2 Stir in the stock, Madeira, and dried herbs, then bring the mixture to a boil and simmer, uncovered, 2 minutes, stirring occasionally.
3 Stir in the crème fraîche and heat slowly until hot, stirring continuously. Season to taste with salt and pepper. Serve hot.

SERVING SUGGESTIONS Serve with pan-fried lamb's liver or chicken livers.
VARIATIONS Use 1 onion in place of shallots. Use ruby port or sweet red wine in place of Madeira.

047 Red Wine Gravy

PREPARATION TIME 10 minutes   COOKING TIME 25 minutes   SERVES 4 to 6

2 tbsp. butter, softened

2 tbsp. all-purpose flour

1 small onion, roughly chopped

1¼ cups beef or lamb stock (homemade
   or from a bouillon cube)

7 tbsp. full-bodied red wine

pan juices from roast meat, such as beef,
   pork, or lamb

salt and freshly ground black pepper

1 Put half of the butter and all the flour in a small bowl and mix together until well blended
   to make a beurre manié. Set aside.

2 Melt the remaining butter in a small saucepan, add the onion and fry gently 10 minutes,
   or until soft.

3 Stir the stock, wine, and the juices from the roast meat into the onions and bring to a boil.
   Lower the heat, cover, and simmer 5 minutes.

4 Remove the onion from the pan using a fine slotted spoon and discard (or strain the mixture
   through a sieve and return the liquid to the pan).

5 Bring the liquid back to a boil, then add the beurre manié a little at a time, whisking
   continuously to blend in well with the liquid, until all the beurre manié has been added.
   Continue to cook, whisking, until the gravy thickens.

6 Simmer 5 minutes, stirring continuously. Season to taste with salt, if required, and black
   pepper. Serve hot.

SERVING SUGGESTIONS Serve with roast beef, pork, or lamb.
VARIATION To make a chicken gravy, use chicken stock and white wine in place of beef or lamb stock and
red wine.

048 White Wine & Mussel Sauce

PREPARATION TIME 10 minutes   **COOKING TIME** 10 minutes   **SERVES** 4

2 tbsp. cornstarch
1½ cups dry or medium-dry white wine
7 oz. cooked shelled mussels
  (shelled weight)

1 tbsp. butter
3 tbsp. crème fraîche or sour cream
2 tbsp. chopped flat-leaf parsley
salt and freshly ground black pepper

1 Put the cornstarch and a little of the wine in a saucepan and blend until smooth. Stir in the remaining wine, then heat slowly, stirring continuously, until the sauce comes to a boil and is thick and smooth. Simmer 3 minutes, stirring.
2 Stir in the mussels, butter, crème fraîche, parsley, and salt and pepper to taste and heat slowly until hot, stirring continuously. Serve hot.

SERVING SUGGESTIONS Serve with broiled or barbecued tuna or salmon steaks.
COOK'S TIP To clean mussels, scrub them in a sinkful of cold water, scraping off barnacles and pulling away the beards. Discard any mussels with broken shells or open mussels that don't close when tapped sharply. Once cooked, discard any mussels that remain closed.

049 Lemon-Caper Sauce

PREPARATION TIME 5 minutes   COOKING TIME 10 minutes   SERVES 4

2 tbsp. butter

3 tbsp. all-purpose flour

1¼ cups milk

2 tbsp. drained capers, chopped, if desired

1 tbsp. vinegar from jar of capers

finely grated zest of 1 small lemon

salt and freshly ground black pepper

1 Put the butter, flour, and milk in a saucepan and heat slowly, whisking continuously, until the sauce comes to a boil and is thick and smooth. Simmer 3 to 4 minutes, stirring.

2 Stir in the capers, vinegar, and lemon zest and reheat slowly until almost boiling. Season to taste with salt and pepper. Serve hot.

SERVING SUGGESTIONS Serve with chargrilled turkey breast, pork or lamb chops, or steaks.
VARIATIONS Use half milk and half vegetable stock in place of milk. Use white-wine vinegar or fresh lemon juice in place of caper vinegar.

050 **Herb & Lime Butter**

PREPARATION TIME 10 minutes, plus chilling   **SERVES** 4 to 6

1 stick (½ cup) unsalted butter,
  at room temperature
finely grated zest of 1 lime

2 tbsp. chopped parsley
1 tbsp. chopped cilantro
freshly ground black pepper

1 Put the butter in a small bowl and beat until soft. Add the lime zest, parsley, cilantro, and black
  pepper to taste, and beat until well mixed.
2 Put the flavored butter onto a piece of plastic wrap and shape into a log. Wrap the butter in the
  plastic wrap, then chill in the refrigerator at least 1 hour before serving. Cut into 4 to 6 even
  slices to serve. Serve chilled.

SERVING SUGGESTION Serve a slice of flavored butter on top of cooked, hot mussels.
VARIATIONS Use the finely grated zest of 1 lemon or 1 small orange in place of lime zest. Use chopped
tarragon, oregano, or basil in place of cilantro.

051 Creamy Fresh Lemon Sauce

PREPARATION TIME 5 minutes   **COOKING TIME** 15 minutes   **SERVES** 4

1 tbsp. sunflower oil

2 onions, thinly sliced

2 garlic cloves, crushed

1 red or green chili, seeded and finely chopped

juice and finely grated zest of 2 lemons

⅔ cup crème fraîche or sour cream

salt and freshly ground black pepper

1 Heat the oil in a saucepan, add the onions, garlic, and chili, and fry 5 minutes.

2 Add the lemon juice and zest, then cover and cook slowly 10 minutes, or until the onions are soft, stirring occasionally.

3 Add the crème fraîche and reheat slowly until hot, stirring. Season to taste with salt and pepper. Serve hot.

SERVING SUGGESTIONS Serve with broiled haddock, cod, or halibut steaks.

052 Plum & Ginger Sauce

PREPARATION TIME 20 minutes, plus optional chilling   **COOKING TIME** 20 minutes   **SERVES** 6

1 tbsp. sunflower oil

1 small red onion, finely chopped

1 garlic clove, crushed

2 tsp. grated peeled fresh
   gingerroot

12 oz. red dessert plums, halved,
   pitted, and chopped

²⁄₃ cup red wine

2 tbsp. light soft brown sugar

1 tbsp. brandy or sherry (optional)

1 Heat the oil in a saucepan, add the onion, garlic, and ginger and fry 5 minutes. Add the plums and fry 1 minute, stirring.

2 Stir in the wine and sugar and heat slowly, stirring continuously, until the sugar dissolves. Bring slowly to a boil, then lower the heat, cover, and simmer 10 minutes, or until the plums are soft.

3 Remove the pan from the heat and let cool slightly, then puree the mixture in a blender or food processor until smooth.

4 Return the sauce to the rinsed-out pan and stir in the brandy, if using. Reheat slowly until hot, stirring continuously. Serve hot or cold.

5 If serving the sauce cold, remove the pan from the heat and leave the sauce to cool completely before serving.

SERVING SUGGESTIONS Serve with crispy duck and scallions in Chinese pancakes. Alternatively, serve with broiled beef, pork, or lamb.

Chapter 4

SALSAS, RELISHES & SALAD DRESSINGS

Salsas and relishes not only add a refreshing finishing touch to many meals, they also add delicious texture, flavor, and color to broiled, pan-fried, or roasted meat, poultry, fish, and shellfish. Choose from a wide variety of flavorful recipes, including Salsa Verde, Red Onion Salsa, Mango Salsa, Red-Hot Relish, and Chunky Corn Relish.

Salad dressings, vinaigrettes, and mayonnaises can be what really make a salad, bringing together all its separate ingredients to create a delicious combination of flavors. Enjoy such classics as French Vinaigrette, Tomato & Basil Dressing, Sweet & Sour Dressing, Raspberry Vinaigrette, Garlic & Herb Mayonnaise, and Moroccan-Spiced Mayonnaise. Alternatively, try a warm dressing, such as Hot Chili Dressing.

Red Onion Salsa (see page 73)

053 Salsa Verde

PREPARATION TIME 10 minutes, plus standing   SERVES 4

1 small onion, finely chopped

2 garlic cloves, crushed

4 tbsp. chopped parsley

2 tbsp. chopped mint

1 tbsp. snipped chives

1 tbsp. capers, drained and chopped

4 tbsp. extra-virgin olive oil

2 tbsp. freshly squeezed lemon or lime juice

1 tsp. Dijon mustard

a few drops of hot-pepper sauce, or to taste

salt and freshly ground black pepper

1 Put the onion, garlic, herbs, and capers in a small bowl and stir to mix. Add the olive oil, lemon juice, and mustard and mix well. Stir in the hot-pepper sauce and salt and pepper to taste.

2 Cover and leave to stand at room temperature about 30 minutes before serving, to let the flavors develop.

SERVING SUGGESTIONS Serve with broiled beef or lamb steaks or pork chops. Alternatively, serve with broiled monkfish or rainbow trout and roasted mixed vegetables.

VARIATION Omit the hot-pepper sauce and add 1 seeded and finely chopped red or green chili.

COOK'S TIP If you prefer a smoother salsa, simply process all the ingredients together in a small blender or food processor until thoroughly combined.

054 Red Onion Salsa

PREPARATION TIME 15 minutes, plus standing   **SERVES** 4

3 ripe tomatoes

2 tbsp. tomato juice

1 tbsp. olive oil

1 red onion, finely chopped

2 tsp. horseradish sauce

1 tbsp. chopped parsley

salt and freshly ground black pepper

1 Using a sharp knife, cut a small cross in the bottom of each tomato. Put the tomatoes in a heatproof bowl, cover them with boiling water, and leave 30 seconds, or until the skins split.

2 Using a slotted spoon, remove the tomatoes from the bowl and plunge into cold water, then drain well.

3 Peel off and discard the skins, then halve the tomatoes and discard the seeds. Finely chop the flesh and put it in a bowl.

4 Add the tomato juice, olive oil, onion, horseradish sauce, and parsley to the tomato flesh and stir to mix well. Season to taste with salt and pepper.

5 Cover the bowl and leave the salsa to stand at room temperature about 1 hour before serving, to let the flavors develop.

SERVING SUGGESTIONS Serve with broiled pork or lamb sausages. Alternatively, serve with broiled or barbecued salmon or tuna steaks, or with broiled or pan-fried portobello mushrooms.
VARIATIONS Use plum or vine-ripened tomatoes in place of standard tomatoes. Use a yellow onion in place of red onion. Add ½ seeded red bell pepper, finely chopped, with the onion.
COOK'S TIP For extra heat and flavor, use hot horseradish sauce.

055 Spiced Black-Eyed Pea Salsa

PREPARATION TIME 20 minutes, plus standing   **SERVES** 4 to 6

1 tbsp. olive oil

1 tbsp. honey

juice and finely grated zest of 1 lemon

2 tsp. hot chili sauce, or to taste

1 can (15-oz.) black-eyed peas,
  rinsed and drained

1 small red onion, finely chopped

½ small yellow bell pepper, halved, seeded,
  and finely chopped

1 red chili, seeded and finely chopped

1 garlic clove, crushed

2 tbsp. chopped cilantro

salt and freshly ground black pepper

1 Put the olive oil, honey, lemon juice and zest, and chili sauce in a bowl and whisk together until
   thoroughly mixed.

2 Add the beans, onion, yellow pepper, chili, garlic, and cilantro and toss to mix well. Season
   to taste with salt and pepper.

3 Cover the bowl and leave the salsa to stand at room temperature for 1 hour before serving,
   to let the flavors develop.

SERVING SUGGESTIONS Serve with broiled or barbecued jumbo shrimp or chargrilled salmon steaks.

056 **Chunky Corn Relish**

PREPARATION TIME 10 minutes, plus standing **SERVES** 4 to 6

4 scallions, finely chopped

8 red radishes, finely chopped

1 small red bell pepper, halved, seeded,
  and finely chopped

1½ cups canned corn kernels, drained

1 tbsp. olive oil

2 tsp. freshly squeezed lemon juice

1 tsp. Dijon mustard

2 to 3 tbsp. snipped chives

salt and freshly ground black pepper

1 Put the scallions, radishes, and red pepper in a bowl. Add the corn kernels and stir to mix well.

2 In a separate bowl, whisk together the olive oil, lemon juice, mustard, chives, and salt and
pepper to taste. Pour the mustard mixture over the corn and toss to mix well.

3 Cover the bowl and leave the salsa to stand at room temperature about 30 minutes before
serving, to let the flavors develop.

SERVING SUGGESTIONS Serve with hamburgers. Alternatively, serve with broiled or barbecued beef, pork,
or chicken kabobs or beef or pork sausages.
VARIATIONS Use 2 to 3 shallots or 1 small red onion in place of scallions. Use chopped flat-leaf parsley
or 1 to 2 tablespoons chopped mixed herbs in place of chives.

057 Mango Salsa

PREPARATION TIME 10 minutes, plus standing   **SERVES** 4

1 large ripe mango, peeled, seeded, and finely chopped

4 tbsp. finely chopped cucumber

2 to 3 scallions, finely chopped

1 to 2 tbsp. chopped cilantro

salt and freshly ground black pepper

1 Put the mango, cucumber, scallions, and cilantro in a bowl and stir to mix thoroughly. Season to taste with salt and pepper.

2 Cover the bowl and leave the salsa to stand at room temperature about 30 minutes before serving, to let the flavors develop.

SERVING SUGGESTIONS Serve with broiled or barbecued chicken drumsticks. Alternatively, serve with chargrilled salmon or tuna steaks.

VARIATION Use 1 small pineapple in place of mango.

COOK'S TIPS When buying mangoes, choose sweet-smelling fruit with tight, smooth, unblemished skins that give slightly when pressed gently.

For this recipe, the cucumber can be peeled, if preferred. However, leaving the peel on the cucumber adds extra texture and color to this salsa.

058 Pineapple & Ginger Salsa

PREPARATION TIME 25 minutes, plus standing   **SERVES** 4

2 cups finely chopped fresh pineapple
    chunks
2 tsp. finely chopped peeled fresh
    gingerroot

1 tbsp. honey
1 tsp. freshly squeezed lime juice
2 tbsp. chopped cilantro
freshly ground black pepper

1 Put the pineapple and ginger in a bowl and stir to mix. Add the honey and lime juice and toss
   to mix. Stir in the cilantro and season to taste with black pepper.
2 Cover the bowl and leave the salsa to stand at room temperature about 30 minutes before
   serving, to let the flavors develop. Drain off any excess juices before serving, if desired.

SERVING SUGGESTIONS Serve with chargrilled chicken or duck breasts, or salmon or tuna steaks.
VARIATION Use prepared fresh mango in place of pineapple.

059 **Chargrilled Pepper Relish**

PREPARATION TIME 20 minutes, plus cooling and standing   **COOKING TIME** 15 minutes   **SERVES** 4

2 yellow bell peppers
½ small red onion, finely chopped
1 red chili, seeded and finely chopped
4 tsp. olive oil

2 tbsp. chopped cilantro
2 tsp. medium chili sauce, or to taste
salt and freshly ground black pepper

1 Preheat the broiler to high. Cut the peppers in half lengthwise and put them, cut-side down, on the rack in a broiler pan.

2 Broil the peppers 10 to 15 minutes, until the skins blacken and are charred. Remove the pan from the heat, cover the peppers with a clean, damp dish towel, and leave to cool.

3 Once they are cool, remove the skin, core, and seeds from the peppers, then finely chop the flesh and put it in a bowl.

4 Add the onion, chili, olive oil, and cilantro to the bowl and mix well. Stir in the chili sauce, and salt and pepper to taste, mixing well.

5 Cover the bowl and leave the salsa to stand at room temperature about 1 hour before serving, to let the flavors develop.

SERVING SUGGESTIONS Serve with barbecued beef, pork, or turkey steaks or kabobs, or with cold cuts, such as beef or ham. Alternatively, serve alongside broiled goat cheese.
VARIATIONS Use 2 red bell peppers or 1 yellow and 1 red bell pepper in place of yellow bell peppers. Use 1 green chili in place of red chilli.

060 Red-Hot Relish

PREPARATION TIME 15 minutes, plus standing   **SERVES** 4

3 cups peeled, seeded, and finely chopped
   plum or vine-riped tomatoes
2 shallots, finely chopped
1 red or green chili, seeded and
   finely chopped
1 garlic clove, crushed

2 sun-dried tomatoes in oil, drained,
   patted dry, and finely chopped
1 tbsp. olive oil
1 tbsp. chopped oregano or marjoram
a few drops of hot-pepper sauce (optional)
salt and freshly ground black pepper

1 Put the tomatoes, shallots, chili, garlic, and sun-dried tomatoes in a bowl and stir well.

2 Add the olive oil, oregano, and hot-pepper sauce, if using, and mix well. Season to taste with
   salt and pepper.

3 Cover the bowl and leave the salsa to stand at room temperature about 1 hour before serving,
   to let the flavors develop.

SERVING SUGGESTIONS Serve with broiled or roasted tuna or salmon steaks, or chicken wings.

061 French Vinaigrette

PREPARATION TIME 10 minutes   **SERVES** 4–6

6 tbsp. extra-virgin olive oil

2 tbsp. white-wine vinegar, cider vinegar, or lemon juice

1 to 2 tsp. Dijon mustard, to taste

a pinch sugar

1 small garlic clove, crushed

1 to 2 tbsp. chopped mixed herbs

salt and freshly ground black pepper

1 Put all the ingredients in a small bowl and whisk together until thoroughly mixed.

2 Alternatively, put all the ingredients in a clean screw-topped jar, seal, and shake well until thoroughly mixed.

3 Adjust the seasoning to taste and serve immediately, or keep in a screw-topped jar in the refrigerator up to 1 week. Whisk or shake thoroughly before serving.

SERVING SUGGESTION Serve with a baby leaf or mixed green salad.

062 Hot Chili Dressing

PREPARATION TIME 10 minutes   **COOKING TIME** 5 minutes   **SERVES** 6

4 tbsp. olive oil

2 shallots, finely chopped

1 red chili, seeded and finely chopped

6 tbsp. tomato puree

2 tbsp. red-wine vinegar

1 tsp. Dijon mustard

salt and freshly ground black pepper

1 Heat 1 tablespoon of the oil in a saucepan, add the shallots and chlli, and fry gently 5 minutes, or until soft. Remove the pan from the heat.

2 Put the fried shallots and chili in a small blender or food processor with the remaining oil, the tomato puree, vinegar, mustard, and salt and pepper to taste and blend until smooth and well mixed.

3 Adjust the seasoning to taste and serve immediately, or keep in a screw-topped jar in the refrigerator up to 3 days. Whisk or shake thoroughly before serving.

4 Alternatively, serve the dressing warm, if desired. Simply return the blended mixture to the pan and reheat slowly until warm, stirring continuously, then serve.

SERVING SUGGESTIONS Serve with falafel and lettuce in pita bread, or with a mixed bean or pasta salad.
VARIATIONS Use 1 small red onion in place of shallots.
COOK'S TIP To save time, use ½ to 1 teaspoon bottled chopped red chilies, or to taste, in place of seeding and chopping a red chili.

063 **Cilantro & Lime Dressing**

PREPARATION TIME 10 minutes   **SERVES** 8 to 10

⅔ cup unsweetened white grape juice

6 tbsp. white-wine vinegar

4 tbsp. sunflower oil or light olive oil

2 tbsp. chopped cilantro

finely grated zest of 1 lime

juice of 2 limes

1 tsp. caster sugar

salt and freshly ground black pepper

1 Put the grape juice, vinegar, oil, cilantro, lime zest, lime juice, sugar, and salt and pepper to taste in a small bowl and whisk together until thoroughly mixed.

2 Alternatively, put all the ingredients in a clean screw-topped jar, seal, and shake well until thoroughly mixed.

3 Adjust the seasoning to taste and serve immediately, or keep in a screw-topped jar in the refrigerator up to 3 days. Whisk or shake thoroughly before serving.

SERVING SUGGESTIONS Serve with a salad of chargrilled or pan-fried halloumi cheese and mixed green leaves. Alternatively, serve with a chicken, ham, or duck salad.

VARIATIONS Use lemon zest and juice in place of lime zest and juice. Use chopped mixed herbs in place of cilantro.

064 **Tomato & Basil Dressing**

PREPARATION TIME 10 minutes   **SERVES** 4

5 tbsp. tomato puree

1 tbsp. extra-virgin olive oil

2 tsp. balsamic vinegar

a pinch sugar

2 tbsp. chopped basil

salt and freshly ground black pepper

1 Put the tomato puree, oil, vinegar, sugar, basil, and salt and peppter to taste in a small bowl and whisk together until thoroughly mixed.

2 Alternatively, put all the ingredients in a clean screw-topped jar, seal, and shake well until thoroughly mixed.

3 Adjust the seasoning to taste and serve immediately, or keep in a screw-topped jar in the refrigerator up to 3 days. Whisk or shake thoroughly before serving.

SERVING SUGGESTIONS Serve with a mixed Mediterranean-style vegetable salad. Alternatively, serve with a pasta or mixed bean salad.

065 Sweet & Sour Dressing

PREPARATION TIME 10 minutes **SERVES** 6 to 8

3 tbsp. olive oil

3 tbsp. unsweetened apple juice

2 tbsp. red-wine vinegar

2 tbsp. honey

2 tbsp. light soy sauce

2 tbsp. tomato ketchup

2 tbsp. medium-dry sherry

1 garlic clove, crushed

1 tsp. ground ginger

salt and freshly ground black pepper

1 Put all the ingredients in a small bowl and whisk together until thoroughly mixed.

2 Alternatively, put all the ingredients in a clean screw-topped jar, seal, and shake well until thoroughly mixed.

3 Adjust the seasoning to taste and serve immediately, or keep in a screw-topped jar in the refrigerator up to 3 days. Whisk or shake thoroughly before serving.

SERVING SUGGESTIONS Serve with a mixed bean or noodle salad, or with a warm stir-fried chicken or mixed seafood salad.

066 Walnut & Parsley Vinaigrette

PREPARATION TIME 10 minutes   **SERVES** 8 to 10

4 tbsp. walnut oil

3 tbsp. red-wine vinegar

3 tbsp. apple cider vinegar

⅔ cup unsweetened red grape juice

1 garlic clove, crushed

1 tsp. French or Dijon mustard

a good pinch sugar

2 tbsp. chopped parsley

salt and freshly ground black pepper

1 Put the oil, both vinegars, grape juice, garlic, mustard, sugar, and parsley in a small bowl and whisk together until thoroughly mixed. Season to taste with salt and pepper.

2 Alternatively, put all the ingredients in a clean screw-topped jar, seal, and shake well until thoroughly mixed.

3 Adjust the seasoning to taste and serve immediately, or keep in a screw-topped jar in the refrigerator up to 3 days. Whisk or shake thoroughly before serving.

SERVING SUGGESTIONS Serve with a mixed bean or garden salad, or with cooked hot vegetables, such as green beans, asparagus, or artichokes.

067 **Raspberry Vinaigrette**

PREPARATION TIME 10 minutes   **SERVES** 12 to 14

1⅔ cups canned raspberries in fruit juice
½ cup red-wine vinegar
5 tbsp. sunflower oil or light olive oil

1 tsp. sugar
1 tsp. dried sage
salt and freshly ground black pepper

1 Put the raspberries and their juice in a blender or food processor and blend until smooth.
  Push the raspberry puree through a nylon sieve into a bowl and discard the seeds and pulp.
2 Put the raspberry puree, vinegar, oil, sugar, sage, and salt and pepper to taste in a small bowl
  and whisk together until thoroughly mixed.
3 Alternatively, put all the ingredients in a clean screw-topped jar, seal, and shake well until
  thoroughly mixed.
4 Adjust the seasoning to taste and serve immediately, or keep in a screw-topped jar in the
  refrigerator up to 3 days. Whisk or shake thoroughly before serving.

SERVING SUGGESTIONS Serve with strips of chargrilled vegetables, such as zucchini or eggplant, sprinkled
with chopped toasted walnuts, if desired. Alternatively, serve with a mixed bean or rice salad,
or mixed salad leaves.
VARIATIONS Use dried oregano, marjoram, or thyme in place of sage. Use white-wine or apple cider vinegar
in place of red-wine vinegar.

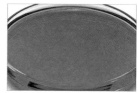

068 Orange Vinaigrette

PREPARATION TIME 10 minutes   **SERVES** 8 to 10

⅔ cup unsweetened orange juice

3 tbsp. apple cider vinegar

3 tbsp. white-wine vinegar

3 tbsp. extra-virgin olive oil

1 tsp. finely chopped rosemary

½ tsp. sugar

salt and freshly ground black pepper

1 Put all the ingredients in a small bowl and whisk together until thoroughly mixed.

2 Alternatively, put all the ingredients in a clean screw-topped jar, seal, and shake well until thoroughly mixed.

3 Adjust the seasoning to taste and serve immediately, or keep in a screw-topped jar in the refrigerator up to 3 days. Whisk or shake thoroughly before serving.

SERVING SUGGESTIONS Serve with a carrot, cracked wheat, couscous, or mixed dark leaf salad.
VARIATION Use freshly squeezed orange juice, if preferred.

069 Moroccan-Spiced Mayonnaise

PREPARATION TIME 20 minutes   **COOKING TIME** 2 minutes   **SERVES** 6

3 tbsp. tomato juice

½ tsp. each ground cumin, ground
   coriander, paprika, turmeric, cinnamon,
   and ginger

1 garlic clove, crushed (optional)

6 tbsp. Mayonnaise (see page 25)

4 tbsp. plain yogurt

2 to 3 tbsp. chopped cilantro

salt and freshly ground black pepper

1 Put the tomato juice, ground spices, and garlic, if using, in a small saucepan and cook slowly
    2 minutes, stirring continuously. Remove the pan from the heat and set aside to cool.
2 Put the mayonnaise, yogurt, spice mixture, and chopped cilantro in a small bowl and stir to mix
    thoroughly. Season to taste with salt and pepper.
3 Serve immediately, or cover and leave to stand in a cool place about 30 minutes before serving.
    Store in a covered container in the refrigerator up to 1 day. Serve cold.

SERVING SUGGESTIONS Serve with cold cooked new potatoes, or with a mixed bean, rice, or pasta salad.
VARIATION Increase the ground spices to 1 teaspoon each for a more pronounced spicy flavor.

070 Garlic & Herb Mayonnaise

PREPARATION TIME 10 minutes   **SERVES** 6 to 8

1 recipe quantity Mayonnaise
  (see page 25)
1 garlic clove, crushed

2 tbsp. chopped mixed herbs, such as
  parsley, chives, basil, and oregano
salt and freshly ground black pepper

1 Make the mayonnaise according to the directions given, adding the garlic with the egg yolks.
2 Fold the mixed herbs into the garlic mayonnaise just before serving. Season to taste with salt
   and pepper.
3 Serve immediately, or cover and chill until required. Store in a covered container in the
   refrigerator up to 2 days. Serve cold.

SERVING SUGGESTIONS Serve with roasted or chargrilled mixed Mediterranean vegetables. Alternatively,
serve with cold, sliced coolked pork or ham, salami, or smoked turkey or mackerel fillets.
COOK'S TIP Garlic is available all year around because it can be dried and stored successfully. A neatly
braided bunch of garlic keeps well for several months in a dry, airy place.

Chapter 5

LIGHT SAUCES & SAVORY & SWEET DIPS

Everyone loves a delicious sauce as an accompaniment to a meal, but some sauces, although very appealing to the tastebuds, are not so good for the waistline. This chapter enables you to enjoy lighter, healthier versions of classic sauces, such as Light Béchamel Sauce, Light Thousand Island Sauce, and Light Red Wine Sauce.

A great way to entertain family and friends at a party is to serve a tempting selection of flavorful homemade dips, such as Red Pepper Hummus and Creamy Garlic & Chive Dip, with fresh vegetable crudités, warm pita bread fingers, breadsticks, or tortilla chips for dipping. For sweet dips, such as Honey-Yogurt Dip and Wicked Chocolate Fondue, serve with a selection of prepared fresh fruit, squares of fudge, marshmallows, or fingers of chocolate brownies.

Spicy Roast Eggplant Dip (see page 105)

071 **Light Béchamel Sauce**

PREPARATION TIME 35 minutes, plus standing   **COOKING TIME** 10 minutes   **SERVES** 4

1 small onion or 2 shallots, sliced

1 small carrot, sliced

½ celery stick, roughly chopped

1 bay leaf

6 black peppercorns

several parsley stems

1¼ cups 2% milk

2 tbsp. reduced-fat spread

3 tbsp. all-purpose flour

salt and freshly ground black pepper

1 Put the onion, carrot, celery, bay leaf, peppercorns, and parsley in a saucepan with the milk and bring slowly to a boil. Remove the pan from the heat and set aside 30 minutes to infuse.

2 Strain the mixture into a pitcher, reserving the milk and discarding the contents of the sieve. Melt the reduced-fat spread in a small pan over low heat, then stir in the flour and cook slowly 1 minute, stirring.

3 Remove the pan from the heat and gradually whisk in the infused milk. Return the pan to the heat and bring slowly to a boil, whisking continuously, until the sauce is thick and smooth. Simmer 2 to 3 minutes, stirring. Season to taste with salt and pepper. Serve hot.

SERVING SUGGESTIONS Serve with chargrilled skinless chicken or turkey breast, broiled cod or haddock fillets, or braised celery or baby fava beans.
VARIATIONS Just before serving, stir in ½ cup grated reduced-fat sharp cheddar or 2 to 3 tablespoons chopped parsley.

072 Light Tarragon Sauce

PREPARATION TIME 5 minutes   **COOKING TIME** 10 minutes   **SERVES** 6

2 tbsp. reduced-fat spread

3 tbsp. all-purpose flour

1¼ cups vegetable or chicken stock
   (homemade or from a bouillon cube), cool

⅔ cup 2% milk

1 tbsp. tarragon vinegar

1 tbsp. chopped tarragon

2 tsp. French or Dijon mustard

½ cup finely grated reduced-fat sharp
   cheddar cheese

salt and freshly ground black pepper

1 Put the reduced-fat spread, flour, stock, and milk in a small saucepan. Heat slowly, whisking continuously, until the sauce comes to a boil and is thick and smooth. Simmer 3 to 4 minutes, stirring continuously.

2 Stir in the vinegar, tarragon, and mustard and reheat slowly until hot, stirring.

3 Remove the pan from the heat and stir in the cheddar until it melts. Season to taste with salt and pepper. Serve hot.

SERVING SUGGESTION Serve with chargrilled or roasted skinless chicken breasts.

073 **Quick Tomato Sauce**

PREPARATION TIME 10 minutes   **COOKING TIME** 25 minutes   **SERVES** 6

3 tbsp. reduced-fat spread

1 onion, finely chopped

1 can (15-oz.) crushed tomatoes

1 tbsp. tomato paste

1 tsp. dried herbes de Provence

4 tbsp. dry white wine

salt and freshly ground black pepper

1 Melt the reduced-fat spread in a saucepan over low heat. Add the onion and fry gently 5 minutes, stirring occasionally.

2 Add the tomatoes, tomato paste, dried herbs, and salt and pepper to taste and mix well.

3 Bring almost to a boil and stir in the wine, then bring to a boil, lower the heat, and simmer, uncovered, 15 to 20 minutes, or until the sauce is thick, stirring occasionally. Serve hot.

SERVING SUGGESTIONS Serve with chargrilled or barbecued tuna or salmon steaks. Alternatively, serve with poached or roasted cod or haddock fillets, skinless chicken breasts, or broiled polenta slices.

VARIATIONS Add 1 crushed garlic clove to the tomato sauce, if desired. Cook the garlic with the onion and continue as above. Use 1 red onion or 4 shallots in place of the yellow onion. Use 1 tablespoon chopped mixed herbs in place of dried herbs.

COOK'S TIP If you prefer a smoother sauce, remove the pan from the heat and leave the cooked sauce to cool slightly, then puree the sauce in a blender or food processor until smooth. Return the sauce to the rinsed-out pan and reheat slowly before serving.

074 Light Green Peppercorn Sauce

PREPARATION TIME 5 minutes   **COOKING TIME** 10 minutes   **SERVES** 4 to 6

1 tbsp. reduced-fat spread

2 tbsp. all-purpose flour

⅔ cup vegetable stock (homemade or from
    a bouillon cube), cool

⅔ cup 2% milk

1 tbsp. green peppercorns in brine, drained
    and chopped or crushed

¼ cup finely grated smoked hard cheese

salt and freshly ground black pepper

1. Put the reduced-fat spread, flour, stock, and milk in a small saucepan. Heat slowly, whisking continuously, until the sauce comes to a boil and is thick and smooth. Lower the heat and simmer 3 to 4 minutes, stirring continuously.

2. Remove the pan from the heat and stir in the peppercorns, then stir in the cheese until it melts. Season to taste with salt and pepper. Serve hot.

SERVING SUGGESTIONS Serve with broiled skinless chicken or turkey breast. Alternatively, serve with poached salmon, cod, or haddock steaks.
VARIATIONS Use extra milk in place of stock. Use sharp cheddar, Swiss, or Gruyère cheese in place of smoked cheese.
COOK'S TIP Black, white, and green peppercorns all come from the fruit of the same tropical Asian vine, but are picked at different stages and processed differently, which affects their flavor. Black peppercorns have the strongest flavor, followed by white peppercorns, then green.

075 **Light Thousand Island Sauce**

PREPARATION TIME 10 minutes, plus standing   **SERVES** 8 to 10

1¼ cups reduced-calorie mayonnaise
4 tbsp. plain yogurt
2 tbsp. tomato ketchup
3 tbsp. drained and finely chopped gherkins
2 tbsp. seeded and finely chopped
   red bell pepper

2 tbsp. seeded and finely chopped
   green or yellow bell pepper
1 tbsp. chopped parsley or cilantro
salt and freshly ground black pepper

1 Put the mayonnaise, yogurt, and ketchup in a bowl and stir to mix. Add the gherkins, peppers, and parsley and mix well. Season to taste with salt and pepper.

2 Cover and leave in a cool place about 30 minutes before serving, to let the flavors develop. Serve cold.

SERVING SUGGESTIONS Serve with cold cooked shrimp or a cold cooked mixed seafood salad.
VARIATIONS Use chopped stuffed or green olives in place of green or yellow bell pepper. Add 1 to 2 shelled and mashed or finely chopped hard-boiled eggs to the sauce, if desired.

076 **Light Espagnole Sauce**

PREPARATION TIME 15 minutes   **COOKING TIME** 1¼ hours   **SERVES** 4 to 6

2 tbsp. reduced-fat spread
1 slice thick or Canadian bacon, finely chopped
2 shallots, finely chopped
1 small carrot, finely chopped
1 cup finely chopped cremini mushrooms
3 tbsp. all-purpose flour

2¼ cups beef stock (homemade or from a bouillon cube)
1 dried bouquet garni
4 black peppercorns
1 bay leaf
2 tbsp. tomato paste
salt and freshly ground black pepper

1 Melt the reduced-fat spread in a saucepan over low heat, then add the bacon and gently fry 2 minutes, stirring. Add the shallots, carrot, and mushrooms and cook slowly 8 to 10 minutes, or until light brown, stirring occasionally.

2 Stir in the flour and cook slowly until light brown, stirring continuously, then remove the pan from the heat and gradually stir in the stock.

3 Add the bouquet garni, peppercorns, bay leaf, tomato paste, and salt and pepper to taste, then return the pan to the heat and bring slowly to a boil, stirring, until the mixture is thick. Cover and simmer 1 hour, stirring the sauce occasionally.

4 Strain the sauce through a sieve into a bowl, then remove and discard the bouquet garni and push the pulp through the sieve. Return the sauce to the rinsed-out pan and discard the contents of the sieve. Reheat the sauce slowly until hot, stirring, then adjust the seasoning to taste. Serve hot.

SERVING SUGGESTIONS Serve with broiled or roast lean beef, lamb, venison, or pheasant.

077 Light Red Wine Sauce

PREPARATION TIME 10 minutes   **COOKING TIME** 15 minutes   **SERVES** 6

2 tbsp. reduced-fat spread
1 small red onion, coarsely grated
1 garlic clove, crushed
3 tbsp. all-purpose flour
¾ cup pinot noir or other red wine

1 cup beef stock (homemade or from a bouillon cube)
2 tsp. chopped thyme
1 tbsp. freshly squeezed lemon juice
salt and freshly ground black pepper

1 Melt the reduced-fat spread in a saucepan over low heat. Add the onion and garlic and fry gently 5 minutes, or until soft, stirring occasionally.

2 Stir in the flour and cook 1 minute, stirring, then remove the pan from the heat and gradually stir in the wine and stock. Return the pan to the heat and bring slowly to a boil, stirring or whisking continuously, until the sauce thickens. Simmer 2 to 3 minutes, stirring.

3 Stir in the thyme and lemon juice and season to taste with salt and pepper. Serve hot.

SERVING SUGGESTIONS Serve with broiled or roast lean beef, lamb, pork, or low-fat sausages.
VARIATIONS Use 2 shallots in place of onion. For a white-wine sauce, use chicken or fish stock and medium-dry white wine in place of beef stock and red wine, and serve it with broiled chicken breasts.

078 **Minted Applesauce**

PREPARATION TIME 10 minutes   **COOKING TIME** 15 minutes   **SERVES** 4 to 6

1 small onion, finely chopped

3 cups peeled, cored, and sliced cooking apples

small bunch mint leaves, finely chopped

2 tbsp. granulated sugar or light soft brown sugar, or to taste

1 Put the onion and apples in a saucepan with 2 tablespoons water. Cover and cook slowly about 10 minutes, until the apples and onion are soft, stirring occasionally.

2 Remove the pan from the heat and mash the apples and onion lightly to form a pulp.

3 Stir in the mint and sugar, then reheat slowly, stirring continuously, until the sugar dissolves. Taste, and add a little more sugar, if desired. Serve hot or cold. If serving cold, remove the pan from the heat and set aside to cool completely, then serve.

SERVING SUGGESTIONS Serve with hot or cold roast or broiled lean ham or smoked pork, or pork chops.

079 Red Pepper Hummus

PREPARATION TIME 10 minutes   **SERVES** 8 to 10

1 can (15-oz.) chickpeas, rinsed and
   drained
4 oz. roasted red bell peppers in oil (drained
   weight), drained and patted dry
1 large garlic clove, crushed
1 tbsp. freshly squeezed lemon juice

4 tbsp. extra-virgin olive oil, plus extra
   (optional) for drizzling
2 tbsp. light tahini
½ tsp. cayenne pepper, or to taste
salt and freshly ground black pepper

1 Put the chickpeas, red peppers, and garlic in a small blender or food processor and blend to mix.
2 Add the lemon juice, olive oil, tahini, cayenne, and salt and pepper to taste and blend until
   smooth and well mixed. Adjust the seasoning to taste.
3 Transfer the mixture to a bowl and drizzle with a little extra oil, if desired. Serve.

SERVING SUGGESTIONS Serve with breadsticks or vegetable crudités, such as zucchini, celery sticks,
scallions, and baby corn cobs.

080 Creamy Garlic & Chive Dip

PREPARATION TIME 5 minutes   **SERVES** 6

⅔ cup sour cream
⅔ cup plain yogurt
2 garlic cloves, crushed
2 shallots, finely chopped (optional)

2 to 3 tbsp. snipped chives, plus extra
  (optional) to serve
salt and freshly ground black pepper

1 Put the sour cream and yogurt in a bowl and mix until well blended.
2 Add the garlic, shallots, if using, and snipped chives and mix well. Season to taste with salt
  and pepper.
3 Transfer the mixture to a serving bowl and serve immediately, or cover and chill until ready
  to serve. Sprinkle with snipped chives, if desired, just before serving.

SERVING SUGGESTIONS Serve with broiled or pan-fried strips of breaded white fish or chicken.
Alternatively, serve with potato wedges.
VARIATIONS Use crème fraîche or Greek yogurt in place of sour cream. Use ½ small red onion or 2 scallions
in place of shallots. Use other chopped herbs, such as parsley or mixed herbs in place of chives.
COOK'S TIP Chive flowers create an attractive garnish for this dip.

081 **Watercress–Cheese Dip**

PREPARATION TIME 10 minutes, plus chilling   **SERVES** 6 to 8

1 cup full-fat cream cheese

3 tbsp. crème fraîche

1 cup finely chopped watercress

1 garlic clove, crushed

salt and freshly ground black pepper

1 Put the cream cheese in a bowl and stir until a little softer. Stir in the crème fraîche until well combined.

2 Stir in the watercress and garlic, then season to taste with salt and pepper.

3 Cover the bowl and chill the dip at least 1 hour before serving, to let the flavors develop.

SERVING SUGGESTIONS Serve with breadsticks, crackers, or a selection of vegetable crudités. Or spread on toasted bagels and top with smoked salmon or trout.

VARIATIONS Use sour cream in place of crème fraîche.

082 Spicy Roast Eggplant Dip

PREPARATION TIME 20 minutes, plus cooling   **COOKING TIME** 30 to 45 minutes   **SERVES** 6

2 eggplants, cut into chunks
   or large dice
1 onion, sliced
2 garlic cloves, thinly sliced
⅔ cup tomato juice

1 tsp. each cayenne pepper, ground
   coriander, and ground cumin
2 tbsp. olive oil
juice of 1 lemon
salt and freshly ground black pepper

1 Preheat the oven to 400°F. Put all the ingredients in a nonstick roasting pan and toss together
   to mix well. Cover with foil and bake 30 to 45 minutes, until the vegetables are cooked and
   tender, stirring once or twice.
2 Remove the pan from the oven and set aside to cool, leaving the foil on.
3 Once cool, puree the mixture in a blender or food processor until smooth and well mixed. Adjust
   the seasoning to taste, transfer the mixture to a bowl, cover, and chill until ready to serve.

SERVING SUGGESTIONS Serve with a selection of warm Middle Eastern flatbreads cut into fingers
or triangles, and vegetable crudités, such as carrot and bell pepper sticks.
VARIATIONS Use 1 red chili, seeded and finely chopped, in place of cayenne. Use 2 leeks, trimmed and
washed, in place of onion. Use lime or orange juice in place of lemon juice.

083 Creamy Crab Dip

PREPARATION TIME 20 minutes   **SERVES** 8 to 10

1 cup full-fat cream cheese
2 tbsp. Mayonnaise (see page 25)
2 tsp. freshly squeezed lemon juice
½ small red bell pepper, seeded and
  finely chopped
2 scallions, finely chopped

1 garlic clove, crushed
1½ cups drained and flaked canned white
  crabmeat
2 tbsp. chopped parsley
salt and freshly ground black pepper

1 Put the cream cheese in a small bowl and beat until a little softer. Stir in the mayonnaise and
  lemon juice until smooth.
2 Add the red pepper, scallions, and garlic and mix well. Add the crabmeat and parsley and stir
  to mix. Season to taste with salt and pepper.
3 Serve immediately, or cover and chill until required.

SERVING SUGGESTIONS Serve with breadsticks, small crackers, or a selection of vegetable crudités, such
as celery and carrot sticks, baby corn cobs, and broccoli florets.

084 Honey–Yogurt Dip

PREPARATION TIME 5 minutes   **SERVES** 6 to 8

1 cup plain Greek yogurt
½ cup thick plain "live" yogurt

2 tbsp. thick honey, or to taste
½ tsp. cinnamon

1 Put the Greek and "live" yogurts in a bowl and fold gently together.
2 Fold in the honey and cinnamon, mixing gently until combined. Serve immediately.

SERVING SUGGESTIONS Serve with prepared fruit, such as apple and pear wedges, peach or nectarine slices, chunks of banana (brushed with lemon juice to prevent browning), and whole strawberries and raspberries.
VARIATIONS Use maple syrup in place of honey. Use pumpkin pie spice or ground ginger in place of cinnamon.
COOK'S TIP Use thin honey rather than thick honey for this recipe, as it is easier to combine with yogurt.

085 Wicked Chocolate Fondue

PREPARATION TIME 5 minutes   **COOKING TIME** 10 minutes   **SERVES** 4

8 oz. good-quality semisweet chocolate,
  broken into squares
4 tbsp. butter, diced

⅔ cup heavy cream
2 tbsp. light corn syrup
2 tbsp. brandy (optional)

1 Put the chocolate, butter, cream, and corn syrup in a heatproof serving bowl. Put the bowl over a pan of simmering water and heat until the ingredients melt and are blended and smooth, stirring occasionally. Stir in the brandy, if using, mixing well.

2 Put the bowl of hot chocolate fondue on a heatproof mat on the table. Alternatively, pour the chocolate fondue into a fondue pan and set the pan over the fondue burner (over very low heat) at the table. Serve immediately.

SERVING SUGGESTIONS Dip prepared fresh fruit, such as whole strawberries, cherries, pineapple chunks, and apricot slices, in the chocolate fondue, using either forks or your fingers. Other foods suitable for dipping include dried fruit, whole nuts, marshmallows, ladyfingers, and small pieces of pound cake.

086 Lemon Cream Swirl

PREPARATION TIME 10 minutes   **SERVES** 8 to 10

1 cup heavy cream
¾ cup Greek yogurt

finely grated zest of 1 lemon
5 tbsp. lemon curd

1 Put the cream and yogurt in a bowl and beat together until the mixture is thick and holds its
   shape. Fold in the lemon zest.
2 Transfer the cream mixture to a serving bowl, then spoon the lemon curd over the top.
3 Lightly fold the lemon curd into the whipped cream mixture using a large metal spoon to create
   a swirly, marbled effect. Serve immediately.

SERVING SUGGESTIONS Serve with a selection of prepared mixed berries, such as strawberries,
raspberries, and blueberries, and lemon shortbread cookies.
VARIATIONS Use sour cream in place of the Greek yogurt.

Chapter 6

SWEET SAUCES & COULIS

Many desserts are just not the same without the addition of an accompanying sauce to tempt your tastebuds. Sweet sauces and fruit coulis often add a special finishing touch to a dessert, providing an extra treat at mealtimes.

In this chapter there is a selection of delicious sweet sauces that are certain to impress your family and friends. Choose from traditional favorites, such as Butterscotch Sauce, Rich Chocolate Sauce, and Rum & Raisin Sauce, or enjoy delectable delights such as Yummy Chocolate Fudge Sauce, Creamy Orange Sauce, and Orange Marmalade Sauce. Also included are a colorful collection of flavorful fruit coulis, such as Raspberry–Vodka Coulis, Golden Nectarine Coulis, and Black Currant Coulis.

Summer Strawberry Sauce (see page 119)

087 Yummy Chocolate Fudge Sauce

PREPARATION TIME 5 minutes   **COOKING TIME** 10 minutes   **SERVES** 4–6

heaped ½ cup packed light soft
  brown sugar
heaped ½ cup sugar
2 oz. good-quality semisweet chocolate,
  broken into squares

4 tbsp. butter, diced
3 tbsp. light corn syrup
a few drops of vanilla extract
4 tbsp. light cream

1 Put the sugars, chocolate, butter, and syrup in a small, heavy-bottomed saucepan. Heat slowly until the mixture is blended and smooth, stirring continuously. Bring to a boil and simmer over low heat 5 minutes, stirring.

2 Remove the pan from the heat, add the vanilla extract and cream and mix thoroughly. Serve hot.

SERVING SUGGESTIONS Serve with vanilla or other flavored ice cream, or with profiteroles or sliced fruit, such as pears, peaches, or bananas.

VARIATIONS Use good-quality milk chocolate in place of semisweet chocolate. Use canned evaporated milk in place of cream.

COOK'S TIPS Choose a good-quality semisweet or dark chocolate for this recipe, ideally one containing a high percentage of cocoa solids.

When storing soft brown sugar, keep it moist by storing in an airtight container with one or two wedges of apple, or a piece of fresh bread.

088 Rich Chocolate Sauce

PREPARATION TIME 5 minutes   **COOKING TIME** 10 minutes   **SERVES** 4 to 6

6 oz. good-quality semisweet chocolate,
  broken into squares
7 tbsp. heavy cream

¼ cup packed light or dark soft brown sugar
2½ tbsp.light corn syrup
1 tbsp. butter

1 Put the chocolate, cream, sugar, corn syrup and butter in a small, heavy-bottomed saucepan. Heat slowly, stirring continuously, until the chocolate melts and the sugar dissolves.

2 Bring slowly to a boil, stirring continuously, until the mixture is blended and smooth, then lower the heat and simmer 1 to 2 minutes, stirring occasionally. Let cool slightly before serving, then serve hot.

SERVING SUGGESTIONS Serve with chocolate profiteroles or scoops of vanilla ice cream.

089 Butterscotch Sauce

PREPARATION TIME 5 minutes **COOKING TIME** 10 minutes **SERVES** 6

scant 1 cup packed light soft brown sugar
⅔ cup heavy cream
4 tbsp. butter, diced

⅓ cup light corn syrup
a few drops of vanilla extract

1 Put the sugar, cream, butter, and corn syrup in a small, heavy-bottomed saucepan.

2 Bring slowly to a boil, stirring occasionally, until the sauce is blended and smooth.

3 Just as the sauce reaches a gentle boil, remove the pan from the heat and stir in the vanilla extract.

4 Serve hot or at room temperature, not chilled. If serving the sauce at room temperature, stir it well before serving.

SERVING SUGGESTIONS Serve with raw or baked sliced bananas, or with scoops of vanilla, chocolate, or butterscotch ice cream.

VARIATIONS Use dark soft brown sugar in place of light soft brown sugar. Use maple syrup in place of corn syrup.

COOK'S TIP If soft brown sugar becomes hard during storage, place the sugar in a microwaveproof dish and add a wedge of apple. Cover and microwave on HIGH 30 seconds. Remove and discard the apple, then stir the sugar well—it should be soft.

090 Rich Mocha Sauce

PREPARATION TIME 5 minutes   **COOKING TIME** 15 minutes   **SERVES** 4 to 6

4 tsp. custard powder

1 tbsp. light brown sugar or granulated
  sugar

1¼ cups whole milk

1 to 2 tsp. instant coffee granules,
  or to taste

2 oz. semisweet chocolate, roughly chopped

a few drops of vanilla extract (optional)

1 Put the custard powder and sugar in a small bowl. Add a little of the milk and blend together to form a smooth paste, then set aside.

2 In a separate small heatproof bowl, dissolve the coffee granules in 1 tablespoon boiling water. Add the dissolved coffee to the custard paste and stir to mix well. Set aside.

3 Put the remaining milk in a small, heavy-bottomed saucepan, add the chocolate, and heat slowly until the chocolate melts and the mixture is almost boiling, stirring occasionally.

4 Gradually pour the hot chocolate milk onto the blended custard mixture, stirring continuously, until smooth.

5 Return the mixture to the pan and heat slowly, stirring continuously, until the custard sauce comes to a boil and thickens. Simmer 1 to 2 minutes, stirring.

6 Stir in the vanilla extract, if using. Serve hot.

SERVING SUGGESTIONS Serve with steamed or baked puddings, or upside-down fruit cakes.
COOK'S TIP Choose whole milk for this recipe, to achieve a delicious, creamy flavor. However, 2% milk can be used as an alternative, to create a slightly less rich sauce, if preferred.

091 **Creamy Orange Sauce**

PREPARATION TIME 10 minutes   **SERVES** 6 to 8

⅔ cup heavy cream

⅔ cup plain yogurt

4 tbsp. store-bought orange curd

finely grated zest of 1 small orange (optional)

1 Put the cream and yogurt in a bowl and whip together until the mixture thickens and holds its shape in soft peaks.

2 Gently fold in the orange curd and orange zest, if using, until well combined. Serve cold.

SERVING SUGGESTIONS Serve with raspberry tartlets or poached figs, or with fresh fruit, such as raspberries, sliced strawberries, or mixed summer berries.

VARIATIONS Use the finely grated zest of 1 lemon in place of orange zest. Use lemon curd in place of orange curd. Fold the orange curd and orange zest into 1¼ cups crème fraîche or sour cream in place of whipped cream and yogurt, if desired. Use all heavy cream, rather than a combination of cream and yogurt, for a richer sauce, if desired.

COOK'S TIPS Before whipping the cream and yogurt together, chill the whisk and bowl as well as the cream, to achieve maximum whipped volume. Use a balloon or spiral hand whisk or an electric mixer, but be careful not to overwhip the mixture.

092 **Rum & Raisin Sauce**

PREPARATION TIME 5 minutes   **COOKING TIME** 10 minutes   **SERVES** 4 to 6

1 tbsp. cornstarch
¾ cup + 2 tbsp. milk
scant ½ cup heavy cream
1 tbsp. butter

1 tbsp. light brown sugar, or to taste
2 tbsp. rum
⅓ cup raisins, roughly chopped

1 Put the cornstarch and 2 tablespoons of the milk in a small bowl and blend until blended and smooth. Set aside.

2 Heat the remaining milk, the cream, and butter in a small, heavy-bottomed saucepan until almost boiling. Gradually pour the hot milk and cream mixture onto the cornstarch mixture, stirring continuously.

3 Return the mixture to the saucepan and bring slowly to a boil, stirring continuously, until the sauce is thick and smooth. Lower the heat and simmer 2 to 3 minutes, stirring.

4 Stir in the sugar, rum, and raisins and reheat slowly until hot, stirring. Serve hot.

SERVING SUGGESTIONS Serve with hot pancakes or scoops of ice cream.
VARIATIONS Use chopped golden raisins, dried cherries, or ready-to-eat dried figs or apricots in place of raisins. Use brandy or whiskey in place of rum.

093 **Summer Strawberry Sauce**

PREPARATION TIME 10 minutes   **COOKING TIME** 15 minutes   **SERVES** 6

2 cups ripe strawberries

juice and finely grated zest of 2 lemons

¼ cup sugar, or to taste

1 tsp. arrowroot

1 Put the strawberries in a blender or food processor and blend until smooth.

2 Pour the strawberry puree into a saucepan and stir in ⅔ cup water, the lemon juice and zest, and sugar.

3 Heat slowly, stirring continuously, until the sugar dissolves, then bring the mixture to a boil and simmer 5 minutes, stirring occasionally.

4 Put the arrowroot and 1 tablespoon cold water in a small bowl and blend until smooth. Gradually stir the arrowroot mixture into the hot strawberry puree and mix well.

5 Reheat slowly, stirring continuously, until the sauce comes to a boil and thickens slightly. Serve hot.

SERVING SUGGESTIONS Serve with chilled lemon or vanilla cheesecake, fruit kabobs, molded fruit gelatin, sorbet, or scoops of ice cream or frozen yogurt.

VARIATION Use 1 orange in place of 2 lemons.

COOK'S TIP Add an extra ½ to 1 teaspoon arrowroot, if you prefer a slightly thicker sauce.

094 **Blueberry Syrup**

PREPARATION TIME 5 minutes, plus standing   **COOKING TIME** 10 to 15 minutes   **SERVES** 6 to 8

heaped 1 cup sugar
2 cups blueberries

juice of 1 lemon

1 Put the sugar and ⅔ cup water in a small, heavy-bottomed saucepan and heat slowly until the sugar dissolves, stirring continuously.
2 Add the blueberries, then bring slowly to a boil, stirring continuously. Lower the heat and simmer 3 to 5 minutes, stirring continuously.
3 Stir in the lemon juice, then remove the pan from the heat and set aside 5 minutes. Serve warm.

SERVING SUGGESTIONS Serve with hot pancakes or waffles, or spoon over lemon ice cream.

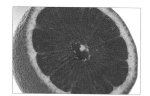

095 Orange Marmalade Sauce

PREPARATION TIME 5 minutes   **COOKING TIME** 10 minutes   **SERVES** 4

juice of 1 orange
5 tbsp. orange marmalade
2 tsp. arrowroot

1 to 2 tsp. brandy or whiskey, or to taste
(optional)

1 Pour the orange juice into a measuring jug and make up to ⅔ cup with cold water. Pour the diluted orange juice into a small saucepan, add the marmalade, and stir to mix.

2 Heat slowly, stirring continuously, until the marmalade dissolves, then bring the mixture slowly to a boil, stirring occasionally.

3 Put the arrowroot and 1 tablespoon cold water in a small bowl and blend until smooth, then stir the arrowroot mixture into the marmalade sauce.

4 Reheat slowly, stirring continuously, until the sauce comes to a boil and becomes thick, stirring.

5 Stir in the brandy or whiskey, if using. Serve hot.

SERVING SUGGESTIONS Serve with individual rice puddings, or with fruit pies or puddings, scoops of vanilla, chocolate, or other flavored ice cream, or broiled fruit, such as mango, bananas, or nectarines.
VARIATIONS Use lemon and lime marmalade in place of orange marmalade and omit the brandy, if desired. Use orange-flavored liqueur in place of brandy or whiskey.
COOK'S TIP Use shredless, fine-cut or thick-cut orange marmalade for this recipe.

096 **Melba Sauce**

PREPARATION TIME 10 minutes   **COOKING TIME** 5 minutes   **SERVES** 4

4 tbsp. red currant or black currant jelly

2 cups raspberries

¼ cup sifted confectioners' sugar

1 tbsp. framboise (raspberry liqueur)
  or kirsch (cherry liqueur), or to taste

1 Put the red currant jelly in a small saucepan and heat slowly until it melts, stirring continuously. Remove the pan from the heat and set aside.

2 Put the raspberries in a small blender or food processor. Add the melted jelly, sugar, and liqueur and blend to a smooth puree.

3 Press the fruit puree through a nylon sieve into a bowl, then discard the contents of the sieve. Pour the raspberry sauce into a small pitcher and serve cold.

SERVING SUGGESTIONS Serve with poached fruit, such as peaches, nectarines, or pears, or with fruit-filled meringues or a Pavlova.
VARIATIONS Use seedless raspberry jam in place of red currant or black currant jelly. Use blackberries or mixed berries in place of raspberries.

097 **Kiwi & Lime Sauce**

PREPARATION TIME 10 minutes, plus 30 minutes standing   SERVES 8 to 10

8 ripe kiwi fruit (about 1 lb. total weight),
    peeled and quartered
juice and finely grated zest of 1 lime

½ cup medium-fat or full-fat cream cheese
⅔ cup light cream
½ cup sifted confectioners' sugar, or to taste

1 Put the kiwi fruit and lime juice and zest in a blender or food processor and blend until smooth.

2 Add the cream cheese and cream and blend until thoroughly mixed.

3 Pour the sauce into a bowl. Sift the confectioners' sugar over into the sauce, then stir in until well combined.

4 Cover and leave the sauce to stand in a cool place for about 30 minutes before serving, to let the flavors develop. Stir well before serving. Serve cold.

SERVING SUGGESTIONS Serve with fruit kabobs, fruit salad, or fruit compote.
VARIATIONS Use 1 small lemon in place of lime. Use sour cream, or plain Greek yogurt in place of light cream.
COOK'S TIPS Use ripe kiwi fruit for this sauce, to achieve the best flavor. Kiwi fruit are ripe and ready to eat if they yield slightly when lightly pressed.

098 Black Currant Coulis

PREPARATION TIME 15 minutes, plus cooling and chilling   **COOKING TIME** 15 minutes   **SERVES** 4 to 6

3 cups black currants, stems removed
½ cup not packed light brown sugar,
  or to taste

1 to 2 tbsp. crème de cassis (black currant
  liqueur), or to taste

1 Put the black currants in a saucepan with the sugar and 2 tablespoons cold water and heat
   slowly, stirring continuously, until the sugar dissolves. Bring slowly to a boil, then cover
   and cook slowly 10 minutes, or until the black currants are soft and pulpy,
   stirring occasionally.
2 Remove the pan from the heat and let cool slightly, then press the black currant pulp and juices
   through a nylon sieve into a bowl. Discard the contents of the sieve.
3 Stir the crème de cassis into the black currant puree, then taste for sweetness and stir in a little
   extra sugar and liqueur, if necessary.
4 Set aside to cool, then cover and chill before serving. Serve cold. The coulis can also be served
   hot, if preferred.

SERVING SUGGESTIONS Serve with French apple tart, hot pancakes or crepes, meringues, scoops of ice
cream, frozen yogurt, or sorbet, or with prepared fruit, such as figs or peaches.

099 Raspberry–Vodka Coulis

PREPARATION TIME 10 minutes   **SERVES** 4

2 cups raspberries
1 tbsp. confectioners' sugar, sifted,
  or to taste

dash or two of iced vodka, or to taste

1 Put the raspberries in a small blender or food processor and blend to form a puree. Press the raspberry puree through a nylon sieve into a bowl to remove the seeds. Discard the contents of the sieve.

2 Add the confectioners' sugar to the raspberry puree to taste, stirring or whisking to mix well. Stir in the iced vodka to taste. Serve cold.

SERVING SUGGESTIONS Serve with mixed berries or strawberries, or with a peach cobbler.

100 **Golden Nectarine Coulis**

PREPARATION TIME 20 minutes   **COOKING TIME** 15 to 20 minutes   **SERVES** 6

4 ripe nectarines, peeled, halved, and pitted
2 tbsp. freshly squeezed orange juice
2 tbsp. sugar, or to taste

2 to 3 tsp. orange-flavored liqueur or
   brandy, or to taste (optional)

1 Roughly chop the nectarine flesh, then put in a saucepan with the orange juice and sugar. Heat slowly, stirring continuously, until the sugar dissolves. Bring slowly to a boil, then cover and simmer 10 to 15 minutes, or until the fruit is soft, stirring occasionally.

2 Remove pan from the heat and let cool slightly. Mash the fruit mixture, or puree it in a blender or food processor, then press it through a nylon sieve into a bowl. Discard the contents of the sieve.

3 Stir the liqueur or brandy, if using, into the puree and taste for sweetness. Add a little extra sugar, if necessary. Serve hot or cold.

SERVING SUGGESTIONS Serve with mixed fruit sorbets or ice cream.

INDEX